UP FROM DOWN

A true story of recovery from addiction

Ted Adamson

WESTBOW
PRESS®
A DIVISION OF THOMAS NELSON
& ZONDERVAN

WestBow Press books may be ordered through booksellers or by contacting:

WestBow Press
A Division of Thomas Nelson
1663 Liberty Drive
Bloomington, IN 47403
www.westbowpress.com
1-(866) 928-1240

ISBN: 978-1-4497-2501-3 (sc)
ISBN: 978-1-4497-2502-0 (hc)
ISBN: 978-1-4497-2500-6 (e)

Library of Congress Control Number: 2011914935

Print information available on the last page.

WestBow Press rev. date: 01/26/2016

Contents

DEDICATION

To all young people struggling with an addiction,
especially Abigail

LUKE 7:40-43:

⁴⁰And Jesus answering said unto him, "Simon, I have something to say unto thee." And he said, "Master, say on."

⁴¹"There was a certain creditor that had two debtors. The one owed five hundred pence, and the other fifty.

⁴²And when they had nothing to pay, he freely forgave them both. Tell me therefore, which of them will love him most?"

⁴³Simon answered and said, "I suppose that he to whom he forgave most. And He said unto him, "Thou hast rightly judged."

Rev. Jesse Lee Peterson Forward for Up From Down

Up From Down, much like the heroin addiction it chronicles, grabs the reader from the first page and refuses to let go.

It's a first-person, utterly compelling look—not just at the hellish life of a heroin addict, but most important, at the motivations that have literally driven Ted and millions like him to do that which they have not wanted to do.

Sin is an ancient word that has lost much of its power in modern times. But the real power of sin seizes men and women beyond their ability to control.

It seizes a person to destroy themselves with drugs, but less discussed, it seizes the spirit with anger and fear, and drives us to use one kind of "drug" or another to quell the pain of our own self-judgment.

Adamson lays this morality play out in vivid detail, and succeeds in showing us how spiritual principles (and principalities) operate in the "real" world.

And finally, *Up From Down* offers real hope for those seeking to overcome the "hell" we are born into, live out, and harbor inside. I love this book. You will too.

—*Rev. Jesse Lee Peterson*

Founder and President, the Brotherhood Organization of A New Destiny (BOND)

Host, *The Jesse Lee Peterson Radio Show*

Prologue

April 1956

I woke up with the morning sun streaming through the bedroom windows, the window frames forming a pattern of crosses on the hardwood floor. I leapt out of bed and scrambled for the blue jeans and T-shirt on the chair, putting them on fast. In all my five years I couldn't remember a morning so grand. The birds twittering and chirping outside my window couldn't be as happy and carefree as I was at that moment. An inner glow of brightness, happiness, and light filled my soul. What great adventure awaited me that day? Then I remembered the new pencil box.

I ran to the nearby desk and there it was. It hadn't been a dream! Grandma had given it to me the day before. It was a brown wooden box with darker swirls of grains running through it in several places. It was only an inch high but had its own wooden handle perched on top, crowning it with glory. Inside there was a long compartment with pencils and three smaller compartments: one held erasers, one paper clips, and the last had a bright yellow pencil sharpener. *I had to be the luckiest boy in the whole world.* I could barely hear the faint voices arguing in the other room.

SECTION 1: DOWN

(The Journey into Corruption)

Chapter 1

"The Pusher Man"

(May 1956)

The day didn't seem much different from any other. The sun was beginning its upward trek above the rooftops and shone on the little house on the corner, still with its blinds closed. The house looked newer, as did all the houses on that street. Voices could be heard coming from inside.

"D...," a loud voice shouted and the front door opened. A man with dark hair, thirties looking, walked out on the porch and slammed the door behind him. He stomped down the sidewalk shaking his head while he fumbled for the keys in his pocket. When he got to the panel truck parked at the curb, he turned around and looked at the house. A puzzled look came over his face. Shaking his head again he opened the car door and put the key in the ignition. After a brief grind the engine roared to life and the truck pulled away from the curb.

Inside the house two young boys, still in their pajamas, were on the floor playing with blocks shaped like large Cheerios. A woman with dark hair and a sharp nose charged into the bedroom.

"I told you kids not to play with those d..... blocks!"

"Run!" said the younger blond-haired boy as he scurried around the woman's legs and headed into the kitchen. The woman wheeled around and took off after him. The older dark-haired boy fled in the other direction to the living room.

The screams and wails coming from the corner of the kitchen couldn't be heard outside the house, but the dark-haired boy could hear them clearly, until the eerie silence came. After a few minutes, the silence was broken when the woman came careening wildly through doorway into the living room in a violent, seething rage.

"Now it's your turn," she yelled. The woman grabbed and held the dark-haired boy tightly by one arm and hit him with full force on the butt. The boy looked up into her contorted face with its vicious, inhuman look of hatred. The woman's arm rose up again and again, and the only sound was the rhythmic slapping of flesh on cotton, over and over. The boy looked up from the vice-like grip into the woman's face and his face began to mysteriously contort as the blows landed. Still it continued. Finally, the woman dropped him from her arms and he crumpled into a heap on the living room floor, like a puppet whose string had been cut.

"Now, go to your room," the woman said sternly. The little boy picked himself up off the carpet and pattered off to his room, closing the door behind him.

The sun was setting behind the rooftops when the panel truck pulled up to the curb. The man walked up the sidewalk and opened the front door. The little boy looked up with sudden hope, saw him coming through the front door and ran to meet him, but the woman was there first.

"The children have been really bad today," she said.

Without hesitation, the man got a stern look on his face and bellowed in a loud, disapproving tone, "Go to your room, Ted!"

Alone in the room, he thought of the injustice of what had just happened and was filled with an all-consuming hatred toward both the man and the woman. Quietly he raged against them both until sleep, forgetfulness, and amnesia overcame him.

(January 1973)

I became painfully aware of it when Don came to my small apartment and sat down in the shabby armchair in the corner. He had a serious look on his face. He coughed a little, as if clearing his throat to say something crucial.

"Ted, I'm strung out," he said, waving his hand in a big circle like a man who had just made an important announcement.

I was a little startled but I looked at him and said, "Well, I must be too. I've been fixing every time you did."

Don nodded his head.

"I think I'm going to quit for a while," I said. "I want to get control of this thing." I certainly liked using drugs but didn't want to feel I was totally out of control.

"They have places you can go to for detox," he said.

I was starting to get worried. *What had I gotten myself into? How bad was this going to be?* I didn't like the idea of committing myself anywhere so I had decided to kick at home. *Why couldn't I give up heroin that way?* I had done it with other drugs.

I decided to ask Don the one question we had never talked about. "What is it like to withdraw from heroin?"

"It's not as bad as you think."

"You're BS'ing me." If there was one thing I knew for sure it was that Don was a liar. I had seen movies where addicts were writhing in bed with their backs arched, screaming in agony from the pain. I worried it would be like that.

"No really, it's not that bad. You shouldn't do it, though. Why kick when we can get loaded?"

I expected him to say something like that. When I bought a spoon from him he usually took half for scoring. I didn't like it but what could I do? I had no other connection. I went to bed that night determined that tomorrow would be the day, but not knowing what to expect.

The next morning I awoke and my skin felt cold and clammy. I felt good enough to go to my job as a cook at Mike's coffee shop, the local mom and pop restaurant. When I got there, I went into the bathroom. This was the same bathroom where I had fixed midway through a shift. I went into the stall, closed the door, and pulled down my pants. As I sat there I looked at the graffiti scrawled in various colors on the walls. It formed a multi-colored collage of slogans, gang names, initials, and drawings. Someone, not me, had drawn an image of a hypodermic needle with a black marker, and gigantic black tear-shaped droplets were drawn from the tip down to the bottom of the stall. Looking at the graffiti made me feel people were rotten. I knew I was no better. I flushed the toilet and pulled up my pants.

Outside the stall I looked in the mirror. I was shocked. It was as if I was looking at a stranger. His hair was disheveled and his shirt was rumpled. The face looked hard and there were dark bags under the eyes. That can't be me, I thought. I peered closer at the image in the mirror; the skin on the face looked pale and clammy. I saw the scar under the left eye from the drunk-driving accident. Yes, it really was me.

For some reason an urge to curse at the reflection came over me. I raised my voice, "You b……, you're the one that's been after me." The image in the mirror didn't answer.

Trying to straighten out my hair, I ran my black pocket comb through it, but the unruly mop stubbornly popped back up. I left the bathroom and sat down at the counter to have a cup of coffee before starting my shift. The coffee seemed to help as I sipped from the steaming mug.

One of the waitresses sensed something wrong. She walked up to me and said, "Cold turkey, huh?"

"Cold turkey is a sandwich," I said. She squinched up her face and gave me that "who-do-you-think-you're-kidding" look and went back to filling the creamers on a bus tray, getting ready for the morning rush. I felt weak and miserable and was hoping that maybe Don would show up unexpectedly with some good dope like he had a few times before.

I returned to the kitchen and started working. One of the waitresses came to the window and hit the little bell on top of the counter.

"Hey, buster, why are my orders taking so long today?" she asked. I felt the anger rising up and wanted to throw something at her, but I needed the job.

"I'm not feeling well," I said, giving her a dirty look. What a bitch, I thought. I worked my shift reluctantly and headed back to my apartment.

When I got home, I immediately went to bed. My bones were beginning to ache. The ache wasn't unbearable, but rather a dull pain with an occasional sharp sting to remind me it was there. *Maybe this isn't the drugs. Maybe I'm coming down with something.* I was lying there with my nose running when I heard a key slip into the front lock. The door opened and the harsh afternoon sun streamed into the room. I winced.

"Hey," Don said with a grin on his face, "I copped." He held up a small red balloon, the size of a large marble. The bag of dope had been knotted at the top and folded over. Don had that excited maniacal look in his eyes I knew so very well.

He walked into the small kitchen. It was hidden from my view but I heard the metallic clink and ring of a tablespoon being dropped on the counter.

"You want some?" he asked.

It didn't seem to matter that I had told him of my decision to quit just the day before. Don was the kind of guy who never shared his drugs with anyone. I couldn't remember a time when he gave someone a "pinch" or even left a "wet cotton". I was strongly tempted, but I wasn't going to let this get the best of me. I ran my fingers through my hair, pushing back the unruly locks.

"No," I said, "I'm going to kick. Remember, I told you that yesterday."

"Oh, yeah, I forgot about that."

He went about the business of preparing his fix in the kitchen. I heard the lighter click and hiss as the butane ignited. Don had an unusual lighter. It was about a third of the size of a man's hand with a burnished silver-gold look and shaped like a dragon. When he clicked it, the flame shot out of the dragon's mouth in an upward arc, perfect for cooking heroin.

I began to smell the pungent odor of Mexican brown heroin wafting in the air. I rolled over in bed and tried to blank it out of my mind. Soon, mercifully, the pungent sweet odor faded. Don walked back into the dual-purpose living room/bedroom with one shirtsleeve rolled up above the elbow while a thin trail of blood trickled down his arm. He was oblivious to the tiny drops of blood dripping from his middle finger onto the soiled carpet. He dropped himself into the corner chair and nodded off into opiate dreams. A few minutes later he was jolted awake when his chin fell toward his chest. He scratched the side of his neck and rubbed his cheeks. Then he looked at me through pinpoint pupils. "Teddy boy," he said, "that's some pretty good dope. I left you a big taste out there."

I got out of bed and walked to the kitchen. There it was all right, a big bent spoon lying on the countertop. Somehow the spoon itself seemed larger than normal. Inside the spoon was a plump, dark little cotton ball and a small pool of brown liquid, slightly tinged with blood. Usually he would have used it all, and left only a sucked dry, arid cotton. I turned away and leaned my forehead against the refrigerator. The cool metal felt comforting against my feverish forehead. God, I thought, I really do want it. I kept my head on the freezer door as if communing with it to tell me what to do. The dope was only an arm's length away, and though I wanted it, something told me I better not. I tried to listen to that voiceless voice.

"It looks good," I said. "But I think I'll pass." Every fiber of my body was screaming something different.

"Okay by me," Don said. "I'll do it in the morning for a wake-up."

I got through the distressing evening and went to bed. Most of the night I tossed and turned, barely sleeping. Don was curled up on top of his air mattress in the corner, sleeping peacefully.

I awoke in the morning after sporadic sleep. I called work and told them I was sick and wouldn't be coming in. The whole day was miserable. My nose ran continuously and my aching bones were screaming for a fix. I stayed inside watching TV, wondering how long this was going to last. An old horror movie was playing on the TV screen. I watched as Count Dracula walked down the hallway looking for something as dark gothic music poured out of the TV speaker. The Count stopped at a door, sensing his victim inside. Then, suddenly, he turned into a puff of smoke and slowly the black vapor seeped mysteriously under the door. I turned off the TV and tried to read a little but just couldn't concentrate.

About the same time as the day before, a key slid into the door. Don had that look of expectancy on his face again. It was like a rerun of the day before. I got out of bed and went into the bathroom, where I took a warm shower. When I finished Don was still in the kitchen. I went to bed and fell into a light sleep right away and slept fitfully for several hours. When I awoke, Don was in the armchair, dozing from the effects of the shot.

I got out of bed and walked into the kitchen. The spoon was still on the countertop. I peered into it and there was only a dry wad of cotton where once had been a refreshing brown lake of smack.

That's it!

I walked into the living room and poked Don in the arm. "Wake up." I said. "I want some dope."

He opened his eyes. "Hey, man, I ain't got any. I shot it all."

I didn't have enough money to score. Frustrated, I screamed at the top of my voice, "I want drugs!"

Don looked startled. "Keep it down—they'll hear you next door."

I didn't care whether anyone heard me or not. "I said I want some drugs!"

"There's nothing left. Even the connection is not holding until tomorrow. You're out of luck."

"I'll rip off a pharmacy then," I said.

The maniacal look returned to Don's eyes in expectation of drugs to come.

I had burglarized a pharmacy before. I recalled the last time. I had climbed on the roof of the pharmacy and then dropped into the adjacent store that shared the building. With a claw hammer I had started banging a hole in the drywall. Bits of debris flew everywhere as I hacked away. When the jagged hole was large enough, I had slipped through into the treasure trove of the pharmacy. I ransacked the shelves. It didn't last long, though—as I was doing it, I saw the bright halo of a flashlight through the pharmacy's window. The brilliant beam of the light shone on my pant leg and then a loud voice rang out through the dark night: "Freeze." I could vaguely see a drawn pistol in the dark. The officer ordered me over to the glass double doors and demanded I get down on my knees. After I complied, he ordered me to put my hands behind my head and lean my torso against the glass door. Then he had leveled his shotgun at my exposed midsection.

"Now just don't make like a rabbit and run and everything will be okay," he had said.

But the memory of the experience and the subsequent conviction weren't enough to overcome my urgent need of the moment.

"Yes," I repeated, trying to convince myself. "A pharmacy burglary is a very good idea indeed."

Don drove me to the local pharmacy. I got out of the car and approached the building. It was dark outside. I looked down the street—no one was in sight. The store's concrete side loomed up as I approached the rear of the building where a metal maintenance ladder embedded in the side of the building made it easy to clamber up. On the roof I found a large hooded vent of galvanized metal, kicked off the cover, and crawled into the duct. It was the first time I had ever been inside an air conditioning passage and it felt weird. I guessed they made them that large so maintenance workers could get inside. *They should think a little bit more about burglars.* It was smooth inside except at the seam where the sections fit together.

I saw a light shining into the duct up ahead. Crawling forward, I peered through the louvered vent at the store below.

The store was brightly lit and I could see the vacant aisles and stocked shelves. The vent hole wasn't large enough for me to drop down into the store so I crawled farther along the duct. Soon I came to a larger ceiling vent. I gazed down into the hole. This spot was away from the aisles and there was plenty of room to land.

I turned over on my back and extended my leg so my shoe heel was right in the middle of the vent. I started kicking but it resisted—a dull metal thud mixed together with a clatter of the louvers echoed in the duct. After four good whacks, though, I heard the sound of the slats in the vent clatter to the floor below. I busted through with several more thrusts. Several electrical wires dangled from the vent cover but I didn't give them much thought. I dropped 20 feet to the floor, landing hard, but I didn't care. Nothing was going to stop me now.

The drugstore's pharmacy was in a walled-off section in the corner. I opened the low, swinging door and entered into my Shangri-la. Going up and down the aisles, I examined the large quart-size plastic containers on the shelves. All of the jars had labels and many of the names were unrecognizable, but I did see they were in alphabetical order. I walked back to the beginning of the shelves, running my fingers across the front of the labels on the white, plastic jars. Finally, I came to one I recognized: Amphetamine. I grabbed a nearby cardboard box and placed the three amphetamines jars in the box. Putting it under one arm, I walked farther down the aisles.

Then I spied another name I recognized: dextroamphetamine sulfate. I picked up the jar and unscrewed the lid. Inside were hundreds of orange heart-shaped tablets with a line down the middle. And there were five jars! *This is going to be great.* Into the box they went and I proceeded down the shelf. I recognized another name: Seconal. I picked one jar and unscrewed the lid. Inside, clustered together, were bullet-shaped, red capsules. Each side of the capsule had Lilly in white flowing script and F40 underneath. Oh shit, I thought, I've hit the jackpot. Lilly F-40 bullets! Red Devils! I took three out of the jar and popped them into my mouth. *I should feel better now.*

After I swallowed the Red Devils I started to think maybe three was too many, especially since I hadn't taken any lately. I decided it would be better to offset them with some of the speed so I grabbed the three jars of reds off the shelf, put them in the box, and then opened one of the Dexedrine jars and grabbed four heart-shaped capsules and gobbled them up. *That ought to do me for a while.*

Ten minutes later, midway through the ransacking, I heard a sound like rodents scurrying. But I quickly realized it was the scuffle of shoes on the store's vinyl floor. The police were getting into position to shoot me if necessary. In a panic, I realized I had triggered a silent alarm.

A harsh, demanding voice rang out. "Police department, come out with your hands up." The awful reality suddenly overwhelmed me. I did as ordered but not before I stashed all the drugs I could into my underwear. At least I wanted some drugs to take to jail. Slowly I raised my hands up from behind the pharmacy counter. I saw several police officers kneeling with their revolvers drawn and trained on me.

"These punks work in twos," said the officer in charge. "Start looking for the other one." They were right about there being two of us, but apparently Don had skedaddled in my car. They handcuffed me and led me off to one of the waiting patrol cars.

During the booking process they confiscated the drugs I had stashed in my underwear. I was fingerprinted and photographed. They drew sketches of the "tracks" on my arms. Then I was taken to the back of the jail and put in a cell.

The next day I was shackled on a chain with twelve other inmates and sent off to the county jail. I had already gone through the worst of withdrawal symptoms prior to the burglary so my pain was mostly mental from being locked up again. As the loaded bus full of prisoners snaked its way through the morning rush-hour traffic, the city howled its morning sound, and I wondered if the county jail was going to be as horrific as it had been the first time I was there.

Chapter 2

"I Fought The Law And The Law Won"

The deputies marshaled us off the bus in our chains and walked us into holding cells, which were jam-packed. Other cells held inmates that were departing to court or prison. We were herded in like swine. I stood with the others for hours in the cell, waiting to be processed without room to even sit down. When I got tired of standing, I knelt down and cramps formed in my legs. For breakfast we got a stale cheese sandwich and a paper cup with Kool-Aid.

The stench was horrendous. Sweat, urine, feces, and vomit mingled together to form a blended odor that kept me on the verge of wanting to gag. There was one toilet in the cell for fifty inmates. When I used it, I had to thread my way between bodies and then wait my turn.

We waited for hours in the holding cell.

Finally, we were moved from one holding cell to another. They fingerprinted us, issued jail uniforms, and then led us to the showers. My hair was long so an officer grabbed an entire box of laundry detergent and dumped it over my head in front of everyone, smirking as he did it. I felt like I was less than human as I went into the shower and washed it off. Then we stood in line and were sprayed with insecticide to kill any lice or crabs. It left a slick dampness in my groin.

After the shower I lined up with the others. Standing naked with water dripping off me onto the concrete floor, I felt as if the last vestige of my humanity was leaking out. The overhead electric lights buzzed and glared like they had on thousands before us. We formed two rows with our clothes and meager belongings piled in front of us.

"All right, listen up," one of the deputies yelled out, a clipboard in hand. Two muscular deputies stood behind him silently. "The sooner you guys do what I say, the sooner you will get upstairs and have a hot meal and get a bunk." He walked down the line, eyeing each inmate. He stopped in front of one of the inmates and looked down at his clipboard.

"Are you Bobby Brown?" he asked. The white inmate with black hair looked back at him and quietly said yes. The deputy nodded his head and turned his back. Then, suddenly and explosively, he whirled around and let loose with a karate sidekick directly into the inmate's groin. The inmate grabbed his scrotum, winced in pain, and doubled over. He did not fight back but looked up at the deputy, his face contorted in pain.

The room became very, very quiet. None of the other inmates said a word. The deputy with the clipboard continued on as if nothing had happened. I was shocked— I had never seen the police act this way before. I expected things to be a certain way and this was unsettling. My anxiety level ratcheted up a notch.

"All right, you guys, turn around, bend over and crack a smile," he ordered. He walked down the line inspecting anuses, looking for contraband. After he was done, he spoke to the group again. "Pick up your clothes, get dressed and go to that holding cell there," and he pointed. After I got dressed, I sat in the holding cell and thought about what had happened. I wondered if the assaulted inmate had been charged with a sex crime, maybe rape.

Although I had been in jail for forty-three days on my previous pharmacy burglary, this was to be a longer stay. Upstairs there were fifteen cells to a tier, and an upper and lower tier. Each tier backed up to another, which made four tiers to a module. The deputy in charge of the module had a command post (a large cell, really) at the front of the cell block, separated and protected from the inmates, where he opened the gates electronically. The smaller ten-by-twelve cells had four bunks; the larger cells had six bunks. The four-man cells often held six people with two people forced to sleep on the concrete floor under the metal beds hung on the wall. The bunks were only two feet off the floor but there was enough room to slide under.

After what seemed an eternity, they marched us up the escalator single-file to the large chow hall on the second floor. The chow hall was filled with rows of metal tables with fixed stools. A row of steam tables was in the front and several inmates in brown trusty uniforms stood behind them. Single file we picked up metal trays, spoons, and metal cups. The uniformed inmates placed a dried hamburger patty, two slices of bread, and a ladle of hot mixed vegetables on each tray.

When I sat down to eat, I made a sandwich of the burger. It was dry but warm and I was grateful for something to eat. None of us had had anything except the stale cheese sandwich that morning.

After we had finished eating, a deputy appeared at the head of the table. "Pick up your trays and get in line at the exit door," he said.

We did as were told. Then the line was marched off to the modules.

I was assigned Cell Two in Charley row. The deputy in charge buzzed open the electric gate and I entered the tier. I walked down the tier and he buzzed open Cell Two. I entered.

I saw four bunks attached to the walls in the cell. One inmate in a top bunk was reading a book. In the other top bunk the inmate was rolled over to the wall, apparently sleeping. On one bottom bunk a dark-haired inmate lay and looked at me without comment. On the other bottom bunk was a fellow sitting on the edge. There was a Bible on his lap. He extended his hand in greeting.

"My name's Frank."

"I'm Ted," I said. I shook his hand.

"You'll have to sleep on the floor."

"I can see that."

"It's not too bad. You get used to it."

"I know," I said. "I've been here before." He nodded in understanding.

For the first week I slept on the concrete floor with a blanket and mattress. My head protruded out from under the bunk but the rest of my body was underneath. The biggest problem was the toilet was at the back of the cell and if someone used it, your head was near the smell.

When one of my cellie's was called out on the court line in the morning, I would get to spend the day in his bunk. That was a definite improvement. We spent the entire day locked up except for meals. Inside the cell I played cards, talked, or read a book from the jail library cart, which came around the tiers once a week.

One day a deputy came on the intercom and made an announcement:

"Okay, listen up, guys. I know it's boring back there. I'm going to pipe music over the intercom and open the doors for 'freeway time.' If there is any trouble it's back in your cells and I won't do this again." I could sense compassion in his voice.

Freeway time meant walking up and down the walkway along the tier rather than being locked up all day. Very rarely we were put into the dayroom, a large space where we could play cards with other inmates. But that had its dangers as inmate assaults often took place in moments like that.

The only thing to break up the dismal monotony was chow time. When the gates rolled back and lunch was announced, it was important to get out because the doors closed quickly. For example, one day chow was announced over the loud speaker and the gates rolled back as usual. Unfortunately, though, I was on the toilet. I hurried as quickly as I could under the circumstances, moving hastily to the cell door and pulling up my pants as I went, not even bothering to flush the toilet. But it was too late— the motor-driven cell door was three-quarters of the way shut. It was too risky to lunge forward since I could be caught in the door.

Helplessly, I watched as the door clanged shut. Inmates on the freeway started laughing. I watched as they marched off in single file to chow. I felt abandoned.

Thirty minutes later I was sitting on a bunk when I heard a click of the electric gate opening at the front of the module. A few seconds later a young, slender white inmate with a bedroll was standing in front of my cell. "Is this Cell Three?" he asked hesitantly.

I stood up and walked to the front of the cell. "No, this is Cell Two," I responded. "Everybody is at chow. The deputy won't open the gates until they get back."

He nodded.

"What are you in for?" he asked.

"Burglary." He looked a little shocked like I had done something terrible. "What about you?"

"I had some pot," he said. "Six joints."

I understood. I had smoked dope for years but one day when I was driving down the freeway smoking a joint I started feeling like everybody in their cars was staring at me. The paranoia caused me to give up smoking weed.

"I quit," I said. "It made me feel paranoid." About that time I heard the click of the module gate again and I knew everybody was coming back from chow. Inmates filed past my cell and my cellies gathered outside on the tier, waiting for the door to slide back.

"What did you guys have for lunch?"

"Polish Sausage," said Frank.

I went over to the rear of the cell and grabbed a marker I had stolen when we exchanged laundry. On the back of the wall, I was keeping track of the days of the week and what we ate. It was Friday. I ran my finger over the menu I had scrawled on the concrete. On the row that said *lunch* I wrote in *polish sausage*. It was silly, I knew, but it gave me something to do and relieved the unbearable boredom. Sometimes I felt like screaming.

Then the gates clanged and rolled back and everybody came back in. It seemed like forever until chow time rolled again. That time I was the first one out. I was at the head of the line when we left the tier headed toward the chow hall. One of the other modules was just leaving from the exit door as I entered. I grabbed a metal tray, spoon, and a metal cup. Two inmates stood behind the stainless-steel steam table, wearing hair nets. I walked up to the first trusty and he ladled a portion of steaming sauerkraut onto my tray. I moved down the line and the next inmate held a tong with a polish sausage dripping brown grease— leftovers from the previous meal. I started to feel better about missing lunch.

That night I awoke in the early morning hours. As I lay on the floor underneath the bunk, I wasn't sure what woke me up but I heard noises coming from outside the cell. It was whispering and I couldn't quite make out the voices. I listened intently. Some of the noises reminded me of the scuffling I had heard in the pharmacy the night I was arrested. Out on the tier the overhead lights had been switched to dim and I could hear the very faint buzzing sound they made. As I tried to identify the noises, Frank got out of his bunk and walked to the toilet. The only sound I could hear then was the splashing of urine and then the sucking roar of the flush. He walked back to his bunk.

"Cellie?" I whispered.

"Yeah?"

"You hear something out on the tier?" In the faint light from the dimmed outside lights, I could see his head cock sideways like a dog who had heard something in the distance.

After a moment he whispered back, "Maybe."

"What is it?"

"I'm not sure. Maybe prowlers." He was talking very quietly, almost a whisper.

"Prowlers?"

"Yeah, you know, cops. Sometimes at night they sneak up and down the tier to see what's going on."

"Oh."

He rolled over in the bunk and went back to sleep. I continued to listen. Just as I was dropping off into sleep, I heard something again. I wasn't fully conscious so I couldn't be sure if it was a dream or not. I thought it was giggling. I tuned into the sounds on the tier but besides the faint electrical humming there was nothing. *I must be going crazy*, I thought.

The next day was pretty uneventful and I passed it mostly reading. The day after that held some surprises, though. I got up early so I wouldn't miss morning chow. The cell door rolled back and I walked out on the freeway, leaning back against the rails on the edge of the freeway. I watched as the black inmates in Cell Three stepped out on the freeway. One of them gave me a dirty look.

We marched off to chow. When we got back from chow, the deputy in charge of the module buzzed the gate open and said, "Freeway time."

I was glad not to go back into the cell. I smoked a cigarette on the tier, talked to Frank about his court date, and then walked down the freeway. As I passed Cell Three, I saw the black inmate who had given me a dirty look sitting on the toilet with a grin on his face. The marijuana smoker I'd met a few days earlier— now with an embarrassed, sheepish look on his bright red face— was being forced to do something disgusting with his right hand to the black inmate. Other inmates on the tier peered into the cell and laughed and grinned.

"Got you a woman there, homeboy. Right on!" rang out on the tier as one inmate passed in front of the cell. I continued down the freeway. I felt uncomfortable, as if I now knew something I didn't want to know. I lingered down at the end of the tier talking to some guy I had played cards with before. He said he was about to be released. Then a voice came over the loudspeaker: "Get back in your cells. Freeway time will be over in five minutes."

I walked back down the freeway and couldn't help but look into Cell Three even though part of me didn't want to. I walked slowly past the cell and glanced over my left shoulder. Now the smoker was lying on the cold concrete floor on his belly; his arms were behind his back, bound together at the wrists. His legs were bent at the knees with his feet sticking in the air. There was binding around his ankles and a strap of some sort connected to the wrist binding. One cheek was pressed against the concrete but I could still see part of his face, stained with tears. His shirt was out of his pants and ragged at the bottom. It looked like they had tied him up with strips torn off it. I went back into my cell just as the announcement blared over the speaker, "Gates being closed." They rolled shut.

Frank was sitting on his bunk and looked up at me.

"Homeboy," he paused, "did you see that next door?"

I nodded.

The next day the only other white inmate in Cell Three refused to go back in after chow. "I ain't going back into that cell," he yelled at the deputy. So the protesting inmate was taken off to "Siberia" and put in isolation for his refusal to return to his cell. After he was led off, I heard a whimper from the cell next door.

"You snitch me off, I'm going to slit your throat with this." I heard a slapping sound.

A short time later a deputy walked past my cell holding a two-way radio. A moment later I heard him say, "There's nothing going on in there, ten-seven."

A few weeks later it was back to court again. I was in the holding tank with several other inmates when the public defender came to the door. "Is there a Theodore Adamson here?" he asked. I hated it when people called me Theodore. It always reminded me of when I was a kid and they called me "The Odor."

"Yes, that's me," I said.

"What's the story here?" he asked while holding a thick file under his arm.

"I'm a heroin addict."

He got a wry grin on his face. "Let me go talk to the judge for a minute." He disappeared out of sight.

I waited about five minutes. I was able to buy a cigarette for a dollar from another inmate and was just about finished when he returned.

"The judge says he will send you to the rehab center if you're telling the truth. If you're not, he's going to throw the book at you."

At that time the State of California had a treatment program for drug addicts. The first step was a medical examination at Department 95, which was in another courtroom in downtown Los Angeles. Several weeks later I was sent there. The doctors examined me, saw numerous hypodermic needle marks on my arms, and certified to the court that I was indeed a drug addict.

After the medical exam I was sent back into the holding tank along with a half-dozen other inmates. There was a barred window looking out over the hazy smog-filled city. I peered through the steel bars and wire security screen, looking at the afternoon hustle and bustle of the city five stories below. As several people passed by on the street below, I wondered if there was any way I could somehow get through the bars and jump to the pavement. *What would it feel like when you smash into the concrete?* I turned back to the holding tank and looked at the bleakness of it all: inmates in handcuffs some shackled together, black graffiti, and images of hypodermic needles scrawled on concrete walls painted gun-metal gray. I was filled with an utter despair. Outside the window people were living their lives amidst the activity of the city, oblivious to my small corner of purgatory.

Chapter 3

"Folsom Prison Blues" at CRC

After four months in the Los Angeles County Jail, I was transferred in a bus full of chained prisoners to the California Rehabilitation Center, a medium security prison. It was called a rehabilitation center, but I still wondered what it would be like as the bus labored up Fifth Street in Norco and crested the hill overlooking the prison. I remembered how my friend Jim had gone to the Youth Authority Prison at Preston and returned a Neo-Nazi. And I recalled the conversation I had had a few years earlier with someone to whom I had sold drugs while we were in a holding cell. He had called Youth Authority "Gladiator School." *But this isn't Youth Authority*, I thought. *Maybe it will be worse.*

Through the transport bus's barred window I could see the former naval base with its foreboding three-story "hotel." The double, cyclone fence with concertina wire spiraled at the top snaked around the compound, interspersed only with darkened gun towers, staring at their trapped quarry. An older muscular inmate with a hardened face was in the seat next to me.

I looked out the window as we approached the prison.

"Have you been here before?" I asked, hoping maybe he could tell me what it would be like.

"Naw, don't worry about it, though. It's a walk in the park. My attorney charged me ten grand to get here."

"I had a public defender."

He looked at me strangely. He nudged another inmate in the seat in front of us and pointed to me. "He got here with a PD!" The inmate shrugged but said nothing.

"Well, I hope you're right," I said.

He leaned over closer to me. I could smell the foul odor of tobacco and onions mingled together. He whispered, "What you need is a daddy." Then he leaned back in the bus seat with a smirk on his face.

A hollow feeling of fear swept over me.

We were led to the reception dorm in chains. After they were removed we were grouped in two lines down the middle of the dormitory. A picnic-style bench was in front of each line. A corrections officer with short, graying hair and bars on the shoulders of his uniform stood at the front of the dorm. He looked like someone you shouldn't mess with— 270 pounds, barrel chest, and tree-trunk arms.

"All right, you guys, everybody take off your clothes and pile them in front of you on the bench."

I flashed back to the karate kick at the county jail.

Everyone did as they were instructed. "I want you each to go over to the laundry room door and tell Jose your waist, shirt size, and shoe size." He pointed to the half-door in the corner.

"And take your clothes with you," he added as an afterthought.

Slowly, inmates picked up their pile of clothes and walked to the door. I followed.

"Size 28," I said. "And medium size 10 shoes."

Jose handed me blue denim jeans, a blue short-sleeve shirt, and a pair of brown shoes that needed polishing.

"Here you go," he said. "First class bonnaroos."

I walked back to my place in line. Everyone was putting on his clothes. As I dressed another inmate walked between the benches placing a paper sack in front of each inmate; I knew it was lunch.

The burly officer coughed and then said loudly, "Here's the deal. We had a stabbing today, and nobody is going anywhere until we shake down all the dorms. So make yourself comfortable."

It was hours later when we left the reception center headed toward the orientation dorm with duffle bags of linen and a bedroll over our shoulders. Catcalls and wolf whistles came from the yard as we walked up the corridor to the "hotel." Voices rang out, "Fish on the line, fish on the line!"

At the hotel we took the elevator to the third floor and arrived at Dorm Eleven. The parole violators were led off to Dorm Thirteen— someone in the Department of Corrections clearly had a sense of humor.

Fear began to settle in. I had known fear before but not like this. It was continuous, ever-present anxiety without end. I did my best to hide it. *How did I end up here?* I wondered. That night, after the dorm lights went out, I stretched out on my bunk, my mind wandering.

My heroin addiction had started when I worked at my first job where a waitress who worked there was a user. Although I had never used heroin, I had used a needle a few times with barbiturates. As I was working, the waitress, Evelyn, walked up to the counter subtly. She was very beautiful and I was fixated on her face. Her sensuous lips were outlined with attractive red lipstick. The words floated out of her mouth as if propelled from another dimension.

"Would you like some heroin? It's boss!" she whispered so others would not hear.

It sounded so tempting and appealing. It was obvious she had heard from someone that I was using drugs. I looked beyond her at the restaurant advertising on the windows and the sun beginning to set in the distance. Darkness was slowly arriving. The flashing red neon sign on the restaurant was backward to me, but I could see its flashing message: "Heavenly Garden Salads." I thought of my dad's warning that he would kill me if I ever took heroin. I dismissed the thought— of course I had heard about heroin but it was probably all lies anyway, just like everything else.

"Yes," I said, "that sounds good." My previous use of other drugs had prepared me for this.

So I had my first fix of heroin. Evelyn came to my apartment with her boyfriend. They offered to tie me off and "hit" me since I had never fixed heroin. I watched as she took a spoon out of my kitchen drawer, bent the handle for stability, and began the ritual. First she filled a tumbler with water from the tap. Then she took a dark, purple balloon out of her pocket and undid the knot. She sprinkled the brown powder into the spoon, took out a syringe, and put it in the water. Next she pulled back the plunger, filled the chamber with water, and then squirted the water into the spoon. The brown powder turned into a blackish/brown liquid.

Evelyn stared at the mixture in the spoon for a moment as if having doubts about what she was doing, but then she grabbed a disposable lighter. She clicked it and the blue and yellow flame danced devilishly on the bottom of the spoon. The brown sludge began to bubble and froth. After a few seconds she put down the lighter. A strange, sweet, pungent odor filled the air, something I had never smelled before— it reminded me of the smell of a glazed ham that had been left in the oven too long. Next she grabbed a cigarette from her pocket and broke off the filter. She stripped the outside paper and pulled off a piece of the white "cotton," rolling it into a little ball. She plunked it into the spoon where it swelled up and turned a deep amber color, and then she picked up the syringe and laid the tip of it into the cotton, straining the brown liquid up into the chamber.

The ceremony was complete. Evelyn flicked her finger against the syringe a couple of times as if blessing the mixture, and then asked me to wrap my belt around my arm. She looked for a vein and found one bulging in the ditch of my arm, where she tapped the needle in. A dark plume of red burst back into the syringe chamber like a miniature atomic explosion. Evelyn got an impish smile on her face and pushed on the top of the plunger. I watched the brown liquid disappear into my veins, and then a feeling of relaxation began to sweep over me. I had expected something different, maybe something as powerful as good LSD. I was disappointed, but I was willing to try it again.

The next time I went to Evelyn's apartment she introduced me to her connection: Don. He was sitting in the darkened apartment at the kitchen table in the corner. I pulled up a chair to the table and watched in fascination as he maniacally plunged and stabbed the needle, time after time, into his arm, trying to hit a vein. I could see the red sores and abscesses along his forearm even through the tattooed dragon, which tried to hide them. For a brief moment I got a glimpse of the presence of evil, but I did not deeply understand that warning or from where it came.

A week later I had my second fix. It was powerful "China White" heroin and that is what hooked me. Don got the drug, and I injected it at a friend's house. After the injection I felt a surge of powerful pleasure coursing through my veins. Rippling thrills of pleasure surged within me, strumming my veins with a crescendo of exciting erotic pulses. *So this is what heroin is all about*, I thought. It gave me a sense of well-being and made me feel, well, powerful— God-like. The promise of something great was being held out to me, but it was a lie that would never be kept.

I started to get to know Don better in the days that followed. Heroin seemed to be his life. I remembered asking him one day if he had a girlfriend or a wife. His answer: "I shoot my girlfriend in my arm." And that was the simple, sad truth about him.

Now as I lay on my bunk reflecting on how I had started using, I felt anger rising up inside me. When it passed, I rolled over and drifted off to blissful unconsciousness.

I awoke the next morning to the loud voice of a correctional officer yelling at the front of the dorm: "Reveille, reveille, reveille, reveille, reveille, reveille." I was confronted by a stark reality: I was twenty-two years old and a drug addict with a seven-year commitment to the California Department of Corrections.

I had heard many things about prison from the grapevine as well as seen numerous Hollywood movies. I had seen what went on in the Los Angeles County Jail, and I expected the worst at this new place. But I had learned enough during my county jail experience never to show fear under any circumstances. During my first week at the dorm, an older inmate warned me not to hang around with a certain inmate with whom I had been friendly. "He is a snitch," he said, "and if you hang around with him you're going to get what he gets." I cut my acquaintance loose.

During the first week new arrivals were given assignment interviews. One morning my name was called, and I took my place with the waiting inmates on chairs outside the lieutenant's office.

When they called my name, I got up and entered the office. Four correctional officers sat around a large round table. One man with a pile of folders in front of him seemed to be in charge.

"Tell us about what happened to get you here," he said.

It was just too much for me. I flashed back to the drawn guns in the pharmacy, the karate kick in the county jail, the marijuana smoker who had been raped, and the inmate who wanted to be my daddy. I broke down in tears.

"I'm sorry. I'm sorry." Tears flowed from eyes. "I'll never do something like this again." I raised my hand to cover my eyes as the tears flowed. I don't think that happened there too often because one of the officers sitting at the table seemed genuinely surprised and impressed.

"Why don't we make this one here an early release candidate?" he suggested. Some of the others at the table nodded.

I was really sorrier for my situation than for what I had done, but apparently I had moved some of the committee to compassion. They voted to make me an early release candidate, which meant my time would be cut in half. I was elated; something was finally going my way.

As an early release candidate, my job was to work in the orientation dorm as a clerk. Mr. Carnes was the day-shift correctional officer in charge of the dorm. Mr. Carnes decided it would be good "therapy" for me to sit in on the initial interviews with each of the new commitments as they arrived in the institution. So I sat in on the interviews of hundreds of drug addicts telling their stories to staff. Most of the stories were eerily similar, like people who had all fallen into the same ditch and were covered with the same mud.

One fellow who had been an alcoholic said he used heroin to get over his addiction to alcohol. Mr. Carnes wryly commented the cure was worse than the disease.

I could tell by Mr. Carnes' comments to me that his intentions were good and that he wanted me to see what addiction did to people's lives. But despite his good intentions, I can't say any of this experience particularly helped me. Mr. Carnes did not have the understanding or insight to help me— he merely commented, "You are a strange person" to me, which was no doubt true and an understatement. I can't remember one person at CRC who articulated any real understanding as to why he used drugs, let alone had any idea as to what to do about it. Correctional staff seemed to be equally in the dark.

One of the higher-ups, a corrections lieutenant, had been friendly when I picked up the daily movement sheet before reporting to the clerk's office. So I decided to ask him a question. One morning as I picked up the daily sheet I approached him.

"Lt. Brown, can I ask you a question?"

He looked up from the paperwork on his desk. "Sure, go ahead."

"They call this a rehabilitation center but you guys all work for the Department of Corrections. Where is the rehabilitation?"

He looked at me a little more intently, and I could see from the look on his face that he realized I was sincere.

"We don't know what to do about you guys," he said. "We just keep you locked up and hope you will get tired of what you're doing."

Then he busied himself with the paperwork. I left his office.

That was the extent of the therapy provided me during my stay. Alcoholics Anonymous and Narcotics Anonymous meetings existed at the institution at that time, but they were not mandatory, and I knew nothing about them. Also, I had not yet developed a desire to stop using despite my suffering. And my attitude toward authority was still in need of drastic improvement. But at least I was being dried out from drugs.

During the end of my stay, something happened. At chow time inmates returning to their dorms crowded into the covered corridors. As I walked I heard a commotion. Someone yelled, "Cuchillo!" (Spanish for "knife") and there was pushing and shoving behind me. The inmates on my right started running. The drumming of feet on the walkway echoed off the walls, sounding like a beast in panic.

Someone had gotten shanked in the crowded corridor. It looked like an old western movie where the cowboy fires a shot in the air and the whole herd stampedes. Somehow I made it back safely to my dorm.

The stabbing was a result of a conflict between two inmates, one black and one white. CRC was not composed of tier blocks and cells but dormitories. The dormitories were connected by the covered walkways stringing them together like spokes on a wheel. There was also the three-story "hotel."

It was not physically possible to lock up the majority of "residents" in cells. But they did confine us in our dormitories for a few days after the knifing.

At chow time the tension in the air was palpable and heavy, like the buzz and crackle of high voltage wires with too much electricity. Guards carefully escorted the population of each dorm into the chow hall, looking over us in a stern, menacing way. As I ate I looked around the hall, expecting it to erupt into violence at any moment.

During the lockdown I played Hearts with one of the black guys in my dorm who was also a clerk. We had been friendly. During the game he looked up at me and said, "I ain't got nothing against white people, but if something goes down I gots'ta stay with my people."

"Me too," I replied.

The lockdown lasted a few days. When the lockdown was over, the black inmates filled the corridors. There was no movement by the white inmates throughout the compound. Tension and fear had the institution paralyzed. It was 1973, and race relations in the country were bleak in general, and even worse inside the institution. Everyone was waiting to see if the compound would erupt into more violence. It was at this point I asked one of the corrections officers if I could walk from our dorm in the hotel down to the library. He hesitated for a moment, sensing the danger, and then said, "Yes, the yard is open." I did not have enough sense to realize how very dangerous it really was.

I walked from the hotel down the corridor to the library. Black inmates leaned against the walls, lining it on both sides; many of them were glaring at me. I cannot say how many had weapons. It was much like someone running a gauntlet of Indians, except I was walking. I remember one black guy whispering to another as I walked by, "That white boy has got guts!"

But it was foolishness, not guts. I believed it was safe because the officials had "opened" the yard. Fortunately, I made it to the library without being stabbed. Someone was looking out for me.

Chapter 4

"Turn on, tune in, drop out"[1]

I was released from prison after serving a mere four months. One of the conditions was that I undergo mandatory urine testing for drugs. My arrest time (including time spent in the county jail before being sent to CRC) was slightly less than a year. There had been no real rehabilitation, but I had been "dried out," which was all they knew to do. As I left the sally port (a passageway with an interior gate and an exterior gate) for the city of Norco, I erased the suffering of the last year from my mind. The first thing I did was make a beeline for the liquor store across from the Norco bus station. I was soon drunk and on my way back to Los Angeles on a public bus.

I wandered into a downtown hotel but couldn't find a bathroom, so I urinated in front of one of the hotel room doors. Urine splashed onto the carpet and formed a large pool in front of the door. I left the hotel with the proprietor chasing me down the street and yelling, "Hey you!" I escaped into the crowded Los Angeles foot traffic.

I ended up living at my parents' house again since there was nowhere else I could go. I soon hooked back up with Don and was

---

[1]   Counterculture phrase popularized by Dr. Timothy Leery

shooting heroin, although just sporadically and only after urine testing. This is what heroin addicts' call "chipping" as opposed to everyday use. I lived in fear that my parole agent would catch me.

Before I went to CRC we had financed our "higher education" by stealing textbooks from the local college bookstore and re-selling them to a book exchange across the street. The book exchange never asked questions and was surely making a handsome profit on the books we sold them. But stealing books from the college bookstore no longer worked since one of the security guards had caught Don doing that. We resorted to boosting meats from markets. I constantly stole money out of my father's wallet while he showered, and filched money out of my mother's purse when she wasn't looking.

I stole so much from my mother she had to know it was going on. But she said and did nothing, not wanting to create problems. She rationalized it: "I just thought you were spending your inheritance" is how she put it years later.

One of the more shameful things I did during this time was stealing silver dollars my father had given to my brother. He had a bag of about one hundred of them. I stole them little by little over several months, and sold them to get heroin. One afternoon my brother discovered them gone. As I sat in my parents' living room, he walked through the front door and confronted me.

"You jerk, you stole my silver dollars." His face was red and the vein in his forehead was standing out.

"No, I didn't. What are you talking about?"

He was so mad he could barely talk. "I know you did it . . . . I know you did." He had an icy look on his face, and I wondered if he was going to hit me. He stormed out of the living room.

That evening my dad came home and my mom told him what had happened. His solution was for us to go out in the backyard and settle the matter.

The bare-knuckle fight happened in the backyard. As we circled each other, we exchanged blows under the faint light from a garage fixture. For several minutes it was evenly matched with no one getting the better of the other. I had always been a little bit stronger because I was older, but at this point we were evenly matched physically. Finally, I punched him hard with a fierce right hook and a splat rang out in the night air. The blood trickled out one nostril and dropped off his chin. He got a look of pain and surprise on his face and his knees buckled. He crumpled in defeat. I walked back into the house and heard my dad tell my mom in a low disheartened tone, "Ted won."

A few days later, after a heated argument with my dad, he told me I had to move out. I felt no remorse for what I had done. How could I? I was still using drugs.

While still at my parents' house, I would get up in the morning and disconnect the phone, so my parole agent was unable to contact me for an appointment if I was using. When I left the house, I would reconnect the phone and go to my drug connection. We would scheme and plot ways to steal enough money so we could buy drugs for the day. Moral boundaries were almost non-existent— we would even steal from each other.

Steve, one of the drug addicts who frequented Don's house, developed resentment toward me due to my thievery from him. One day he had Don's little brother sell me some LSD. As it began to take effect, he leapt up and announced that he had laced the LSD with rat poison and that it was a fatal dose. Much to his surprise, I calmly said, "What are you going to do with my body?" I had reached the point where I no longer much cared if I lived or died. There was no rat poison in the drugs after all, and Steve stormed off. His plan to freak me out had failed.

About this time I decided I would try methadone maintenance. It seemed like a good way to get drugs to me. One morning, at my connection's house, I called up a drug treatment center and told them I was interested in getting on methadone. A man on the other end of the phone asked me some questions about how much I was using, and then asked me about treatment failures. I told him I had been to CRC once. He told me they considered that one treatment failure.

"Have you been any in any other treatment programs?" he asked.

I responded truthfully. "No, I haven't."

"You have to have two treatment failures before we can put you on methadone," he said.

I hung up the phone. I was somewhat disappointed that I wasn't going to get any drugs from them.

Pauline, an old girlfriend, showed up in my life unexpectedly one day. She called me, and I met her down at the liquor store on the corner. She was standing outside with a long granny-type dress on. Her straight brown hair cascaded off her shoulders, and her dark brown eyes flashed in the sun. She had that mischievous look on her face that she always had. I had forgotten how beautiful she was. I was very glad to see her, although somewhat surprised. She had been living with another man the whole time I had been seeing her. Perhaps "girlfriend" was not the right word for her. "Shared girlfriend" would have been more accurate. At any rate, I had told her she had to choose between us as the ménage à trois was just too painful for me.

Her friend Sonya was waiting in a nearby car. I got in the passenger's seat. Sonya was the driver, but we just parked for a while and chatted. I was looking forward to an afternoon of fun. After a few minutes Pauline mentioned she had some LSD and offered it to me. I took it, and five minutes later I started to feel its effects. It was powerful. As I began to feel loaded, Pauline announced to me she had to leave.

"I thought we were going to do something. I can't go home like this," I said in a panic. My condition was already too far gone, and it was just beginning.

She looked at me with a face of stone and said, "That's what you did to me, gave me acid and sent me home. Why shouldn't I do it to you?" The effects of the LSD were hitting me, but I could still sense the hatred behind her words.

I flashed back to the last time I had seen Pauline. She had come to see me at my apartment, shortly before I started using heroin. She had come to see how I was doing because she had heard I wasn't doing well since our breakup. I wanted sex but she said no. I had some LSD, and tried to use it as a lure to get her to stay. I said I would only give it to her if she agreed to take it there in my apartment. She agreed, but surprised me by leaving after I gave it to her.

Looking back at that day, I began to understand her hatred toward me.

I was tripping so much that I could do or say nothing. Sonya and Pauline decided to take me to a park in the San Pedro area and just drop me off. I was unable to walk on my own,and had to be supported under each arm by one of them. They sat me on a park bench, propped me up, and then left. I sat there watching a young couple necking. How long I sat there on the park bench I do not know, but it was hours.

Sonya and Pauline had abandoned me, but apparently they had an attack of conscience and came back. Several hours later through a hazy psychedelic fog I saw them returning: two stick-like figures undulating toward me.

"Look," Pauline said as they approached, "he's still here. We shouldn't have done this." They propped me up under each arm again, and I stagger-walked back to their car.

They drove me back to my parents' house but I have little memory of the trip. All I remember is Pauline asking Sonya about the LSD. Sonya replied she had asked the dealer for the strongest LSD they had, and that what I had taken was what they had given her.

When they arrived outside the house, Pauline said, "Ted, just go inside your house. You will be okay." I heard her voice breaking up. And that was the last I ever saw Pauline. She had gotten her measure of revenge, and become exactly like what she hated: me.

I got a job at a plastic extrusion company working nights, but it wasn't long before I lost it. I went to work at another restaurant, but was soon fired from that job too. I no longer had the ability to hold down a job— getting loaded had become my real career.

One day while riding in a car with other drug addicts, we were arrested for "marks" (injection marks on our arms). I went to the county jail, and a parole hold was put on me.

My parole agent, Mr. Schwartz, came to visit me. He had someone with him. During the interview the person with him asked me, "Do you believe in God?" At the time I thought it was a strange question.

"Yes," I responded, "in my own way." Really, I hadn't given much thought to God to tell the truth. As I like to say these days, when you are sitting around a house with other drug addicts plotting to steal enough for the day to fix, the subject of God hardly ever comes up.

My parole agent looked askance at the man with him and said, "That's not going to work with him."

After the interview my parole agent gave me a choice: drug treatment or back to CRC. I choose drug treatment, but not because I had any desire for "treatment" or any desire to stop using drugs. I merely did not want to go back to CRC because of the stabbings and race riots.

Chapter 5

"I don't know how to cure a dope fiend.
I never did."[2]

The drug treatment program my parole agent chose was a long-term program at a psychiatric hospital in Tarzana, California. It was one of the many programs in the early 1970's based on Synanon, sometimes referred to as "Synanon clone" programs. It was called "The Family." I was in for a rude awakening.

My first view of The Family was in the cafeteria as they stood in a jagged line for lunch. They most closely resembled a colorful line of carnival sideshow freaks. I had never seen anything like it in my life. The men all had shaved heads and wore dresses! The women were all wearing men's clothing; one was wearing a worn tuxedo. Some were wearing paper bags over their heads with slits for their eyes, nose, and mouth. All were wearing sandwich cardboard signs with strange crayon-marked messages on them.

---

[2]   Charles Dederich, Synanon Founder, speaking to a US District Court Judge in 1982, Phoenix New Times/October 10,1996 by John Dougherty

It was a weird menagerie of bizarre design. I was shocked and speechless at what I saw. It was like a forced landing on a distant planet inhabited by gaudy aliens. I got a very uneasy feeling in the pit of my stomach. Something very weird was definitely going on.

I went for screening before Family members. It was a small screening committee with two "elders" and several lower-phase people. The elders were not paid staff, but were the oldest residents at the facility. They were in positions of authority, and ran the day-to-day operations under the supervision of the paid staff. The longer a resident stayed at the facility, the more responsibility he was given. The two elders sat in chairs at one end of the room, and the three lower-phase people formed a semi-circle. Their faces were all serious, looking at me intently. I sat in a chair facing them.

One elder, an older white man with a mustache, asked me, "How do you feel about being here?"

I looked up and said, "I'm a little apprehensive."

"A little apprehensive?" the elder questioned.

My fear turned to anger, and I felt my face twist into a semi snarl. "Okay, I'm afraid!" I blurted out with an attitude. I was getting defensive and hostile.

The elder nodded his head and said, "Fear of the unknown."

They asked me if I had a girlfriend.

"I had one but I don't see her anymore. I loved her," I said.

One of the other elders, a black man, stared at me. "How could you love her when you don't love yourself?"

I hadn't expected that. "I don't know."

They asked me about my drug use and I told them about my "runs." Then they told me I was going to have to have a lot of "blind faith" that the program worked. After the interview they sent me to the candidacy phase of the program.

The candidacy was the phase where they observed you to determine if you were suitable for the program. It's difficult to describe what Tarzana what like. It was a combination of modern boot camp, Synanon, and maybe a prisoner-of-war brainwashing camp. Etta James, the famous blues singer (and my phase leader), described it as the "marines of rehab" in her autobiography *Rage to Survive*. She described the basic training as "hell." It was.

During my first night at The Family, all the candidates were rudely awakened at two a.m. by a bald phase leader screaming, "Creep, creep, creep." As I was about to find out, a "creep" meant we were being awakened in the middle of the night as "therapy." Imagine someone walked into your bedroom at night and screaming "creep" without any warning. The shock and surprise were complete.

It is truly amazing what can be done to human beings in the name of therapy. The first "therapy" I was exposed to was "standing on the wall," which was a big part of The Family program. If you ever stood in the corner for punishment as a child, then you have a sense of what standing on the wall is like. The candidates (eight to ten of us) were forced to stand in a line with our noses and toes on the wall. Usually it was from ten to thirty minutes. However, there were times when we stood on the wall for as long as twenty hours or even more. It was incredible cruelty to be forced to stand immovable against the wall for these lengths of time. It was cruelty without lasting physical harm, though— it is astonishing what you can get used to.

When the long periods of wall time came, it got to the point of becoming physically unbearable. The ache of gravity on the soles of my feet resulted in a dull, persistent throbbing, a low intensity ache. Sometimes staff would put us on the wall and then walk off to another room, leaving us there to slowly suffer while they sat in comfortable chairs. Although staff was not there, I still had to stay on the wall. If I left the wall, one of my "peers" would report me to staff. Later I would receive discipline, which was handed out once a week. Discipline could include wearing a dress for the next week with a sign that said "I violate the rules" or perhaps some individual wall time. After a while I realized the best course was just to stand on the wall and take the dull ache.

If the pain became too much, I would ask to go to the bathroom, the only time we were allowed to come off the wall. For a few minutes I could get relief for my throbbing feet by sitting on the toilet. I would walk as slowly as I could to the lavatory at the end of the hall, go into the toilet, sit, and take off my shoes. Then I would rub and massage my poor painful feet in their socks, trying to make the dull pounding go away. I would stay in the toilet as long as I could to give my feet a rest. If I stayed too long, I knew I would be in trouble. Then it was back to the wall. As soon as I got back on the wall, the dull ache in my feet would start again.

Sometimes we were forced down on our knees with our elbows on the wall in uncomfortable stress positions. Then the staff would verbally indict us (scream out our shortcomings, real and imagined) as we stood or kneeled in these awkward positions. This, of course, is cruelty and not therapy but that's what they did. In the beginning I was not told anything, except that I would have to have a lot of blind faith and that the program worked. I acknowledge that the staff, who were graduates of a similar facility at Camarillo State Hospital, meant well, but the methods were barbaric. They didn't know any different— it was what they had been taught and what had been done to them. Surely men like Ronald Reagan (California's governor at the time) did not know what was really going on behind the scenes. I found out later (in Etta James' book *Rage to Survive*) that the staff concealed from the Los Angeles County Supervisors the harsh confrontational attack "therapy" that occurred during the so-called "Synanon Game."

I didn't realize it at the time, but programs like this one in Tarzana were an attempt by the mental health community to mimic the "success" of the Synanon program. These Synanon clone programs were less well known. When I was in The Family in 1974, Synanon clone programs were still popular, but have been mostly replaced by twelve-step programs. The Family still exists and hosts twelve-step programs at their facility. I do not know how their current program is run.

Briefly, the Synanon Game is a combination group confrontation and encounter. One person is placed on the "hot seat" or probe and verbally attacked by other people in the game. Much truth is said but since we are mostly talking about corrupted criminal drug addicts it is mostly or entirely without love. Much non-truth is also said.

I found myself projecting my faults onto others during the Synanon Game (projection is just that: projecting your faults onto others). I remember verbally attacking one poor fellow after he said he loved his girlfriend.

"If you loved her, then why did you give her drugs?" I screamed.

It turned out the fellow I was confronting had never given his girlfriend drugs. I was the one who had given my girlfriend, Pauline, drugs. In some bizarre way I was angrily projecting the sins I had not faced up to inside myself onto others.

Another time I told the group there was a lot of "underground hostility" in the room; it was not until many, many years later that I realized the full extent of that particular projection. The purpose of the game is supposedly therapeutic, but how effective was it to have sick, insane, criminal, drug addicts verbally attacking one another and acting like therapists?

The candidacy phase of the program lasted a few weeks to a month. It was designed, I suppose, as a period where the candidate became oriented, and the staff observed the candidate to see if he or she was acceptable. Many, many people "split" (left the program) during the candidacy phase due to the "creeps," standing on the wall, the Synanon Game, and other "therapies." More people split than stayed. I remember one fellow split, and then we heard several weeks later that he had committed suicide. Addiction is a serious business— many don't survive it one way or another.

One time during the candidacy phase one of our leaders decided to discipline me. Honestly, I can't remember what I did to cause it—if anything. But I do remember the discipline. She had me get a five-gallon plastic container and fill it with small rocks, some of which had sharp edges. Then she had me fill it with water. After it was filled with water, I was forced to stand in the bucket on the rocks with my bare feet. Although the rocks did not cut my feet, it was exceedingly painful; I was left that way for twenty to thirty minutes. In fairness to the paid staff, I don't think they knew the phase leaders were doing this sort of thing to candidates, but it happened nonetheless.

After the candidate phase it was time for my screening into The Family. Screening was accomplished by means of the Synanon Game. I walked into the interview room and was put on the "hot seat." I sat in the chair facing a semi-circle of perhaps twenty drug addicts, including paid staff. They started asking me questions like what I had been doing there. I gave them the answers I thought they wanted to hear. I told them I had been fulfilling the assignments I had been given.

Then, without warning, the vicious verbal attack began. They started attacking me with verbal abuse and profanity. I had never experienced anything like it in my entire life. There was loud screaming, and they started shouting things at me. I was told to sit on my hands. Shouts came from one side of the room, then the other side. There was name-calling, shrieking, and ridicule. One woman grabbed her breast and mocked me: "You want some of this, you little baby?" One of the senior staff members circled his finger in the air, a hand signal to others to keep up the verbal attacks. I started reacting with anger.

No, *anger* is not the correct word for it. It was hatred: a searing, seething resentment, a deep-burning ready-to-kill type of hate. Someone in the room said, "Look at that hate." It was a generalized hate for everybody in the room. I snarled at them and flashed missiles from my angry eyes from one end of the room to the other. Then I exploded angrily at one of the senior staff members in the room: "You can take this whole great big program, roll it up into a little ball and STUFF IT!"

The staff member was shocked. "You've got ten seconds to apologize or get out," he said.

Then something amazing started to happen. They started counting down as a group: "Ten, nine, eight, seven, six, five, four, three, two, one— you're out."

At the time I didn't understand what was happening, but my excessive emotionality had put me in a very suggestible state. I felt like it was a prizefight and I was being counted out. When they said "you're out" it became a hypnotic suggestion to me due to my intense hatred and resentment. I closed my eyes and went "out" (just like they told me). My eyes were shut tight. They told me to open my eyes. I replied that I couldn't, and it was true. I really couldn't. I tried to open my eyes and could not.

I was in some type of emotionally induced hypnotic trance, and my eyelids were stuck shut. Apparently, the group attack and the hatred had produced hypnosis and the suggestion "you're out" made me go into a semi-conscious hysterical state.

It took them a while to realize that something was seriously wrong with me. I vaguely remember them calling some of the staff members at home and saying, "What we feared would happen has finally happened."

I have no memory of waking up but I must have because I remember them sending me out of the room and I came back. They told me I was very sick and they didn't know if they could help me or not, but that they would try. "Welcome to The Family," they said, and hugged me. And despite their faults and the insanity of the program, I do acknowledge that they tried to help me. But if the blind lead the blind, won't they both fall in a ditch?

Chapter 6

The Family

Being in The Family was like being a candidate, only much harder. The Candidacy had only been a foretaste of what was to come. I already knew most of the yellow phasers as many had been in the candidacy with me (The Family was divided into various phases based on length of time and "accomplishments": candidacy, yellow, blue, and elder).

One of the first things that happened in The Family was that I was given weekly commitments or assignments. One of the assignments given to everyone was to "book" people. "Booking" was writing anyone up for a minor or major program violation and turning them into staff, sort of like a speeding ticket. We were all required to book people. Failure to do so could be construed as a bad attitude, which could result in your being ejected from the program— no small thing when you consider some of the family members were facing as much as fifteen years in prison. This is where programs like this got the reputation among drug addicts for being snitch programs. As a result of the booking, the staff assigned discipline.

Our phase leader was Jamesetta Hawkins, otherwise known as Etta James, the famous blues singer. She's made no secret about being in Tarzana, and I don't see any reason not to identify her since she wrote about the Tarzana Family in her autobiography.

And then there were the yellow phasers themselves. They were all drug addicts.

There was Billy, a young black man. We had the same parole agent, which meant he had been out to CRC before. Billy had the reputation of being slick.

There was Caroline, who was older than most of us and had been a meth user. She had been seriously disfigured in a gas explosion at her apartment while on drugs and had told everybody it was an accident. One day while having a dyad (an assigned conversation between two people, given as a result of discipline) she told me the whole incident. She said she entered her apartment, and there was a strong smell of gas. She walked up to the stove, and then struck a match to see what was going on. I realized as she was talking how crazy that was.

"You were trying to commit suicide, weren't you?" I asked.

She got a shocked look on her face and nodded in agreement. I got the feeling she was admitting the truth of what happened for the very first time.

There was my buddy Irving. He had been through the family program at Camarillo State Hospital, but apparently it hadn't worked; he was back for more treatment. We had made friends while in the candidacy. The program staff were always hard on him; apparently they felt he needed it because of his previous treatment failure.

There was Debbie, an attractive young girl with a serious drug problem. She had turned herself in voluntarily, not because of any court commitments. She really wanted to beat her drug habit. She confided some of her dark secrets to me during our dyads, but nothing I should repeat.

There was Tom and Natasha, who were married. They had been drug dealers and had gotten busted. They were facing substantial amounts of prison time. Tom and Natasha had been placed on non-communication status. I forget what the program called it but it meant they were not allowed to talk to one another.

One day I was in the utility room washing out some mops. Natasha was there too, doing some work. Tom walked into the utility room and gave her a hug and quick kiss. I decided to book them for it, and when I did all hell broke loose.

The head of the program called me in his office and asked me what I had seen.

"I saw Tom give Natasha a kiss," I said. Apparently they believed me but they got weird looks on their faces. "It was just a tiny little kiss," I said. I felt like I had done what I was supposed to do, but that everybody wished I hadn't done it. They told me to leave. Apparently, the staff took the non-communication rule very serious. I had no idea that they would make such a big deal of it.

They placed Tom in a chair at one end of the hallway, and Natasha in a chair at the other end. Natasha was made to wear a sign that said "Tom, we're getting close to the big house." They were forced to sit in the chairs from morning till evening every day for weeks. No relief but to go to chow or the bathroom. Whenever I walked by them I felt like I was to blame.

What was worse is that everybody in the program blamed me for it too. They felt it was just an innocent kiss, and I shouldn't have booked them. I was made to feel like a pariah.

There was also Jim, a black man who had arrived at Tarzana about the same time as me. We had been in the candidacy together. I didn't know much about him except he struck me as pathetic. And he didn't seem to like me much.

There was Manny, a gang member from East Los Angeles, and one tough cookie. When he looked at me it was usually with a scowl, and I was always expecting a left hook, which never came. I'm not sure if it was because I was white or what, but clearly he didn't like me.

There were also a few others that came into yellow phase while I was there, but it doesn't seem important to mention them now.

One day after standing on the wall for quite some time I raised my hand and asked Etta if I could go to the bathroom.

"Come off the wall and go," she said.

I sauntered down the hallway to the bathroom, taking as much time as I could. I relished every moment when I wasn't glued to the wall. I stayed in the bathroom as long as I could even though I didn't really have to go, flushing the toilet numerous times. After leaving the bathroom I returned to my position on the wall.

"I gotta go too," Jim said. That's how it always was. As soon as one person was given permission to go to the bathroom, everyone wanted his or her turn off the wall.

"Go ahead," Etta said. I heard Jim's footsteps as he walked down the hall and the closing of the bathroom door. After about ten minutes I heard the flushing of the toilet and heard the door open. I heard Jim's footsteps shuffling down the corridor. He stopped right behind me.

"Ted, you're booked for dribbling on the toilet seat," he said. Everybody on the wall laughed. I didn't know what to say—I didn't know if I had done it or not. It was sort of like a cop handing out tickets. You had to get your quota, and sometimes it didn't much matter if it was true or not. I said nothing.

Discipline was handed out every Saturday morning. We stood in a line outside the elders' office, and then went inside individually. That next Saturday morning I walked into the elder's office to see the two elders sitting in their chairs.

"So you dribbled on the toilet seat, eh?" one elder said. I felt like I had been accused of a murder.

"Well, I don't really know," I said.

"Hmmm, maybe you need some time to think about this," the elder said. He picked up the bottom half of a broken toilet seat by his desk and handed it to me.

"Your discipline for this week is to wear this around your neck every waking moment of the day. And make a sign that says 'Watch out if you sit down after me.'"

Yes, I had been branded with the scarlet toilet seat. After meeting with the elders, we were all sent to the yellow phase room to make our signs and discipline.

When I walked into the dayroom, Billy was there stringing together cigarette butts with a needle and thread.

Discipline could be varied. In addition to booking people, our heads were shaved, and we were made to wear women's dresses or men's suits and the ever-present cardboard sandwich signs. The reason for the cross-dressing was never really explained to me. The reason for the shaved head was also never explained although I know that this had been done at Synanon as well. And perhaps that was the only reason for it. Or maybe it was to humiliate us or strip us of our identity. At any rate the reasons for lots of things were not explained—it was all blind faith, as they called it.

We were given confrontation assignments with other Family members. Sometimes, in the afternoons, we had negative feedback sessions. Negative feedback sessions were when we sat around and told each other negative things about ourselves. There were dyads. Sometimes we were put on "monad." Monad was enforced silence when you are ordered not to talk to anyone and they are ordered not to talk to you for a period of time— sometimes for many days or even weeks. And we played the Synanon game usually about once a week.

We were made to run laps, endlessly, at the back of the facility. We also were subject to very, very severe sleep deprivation. Many nights we only slept a couple of hours, and then spent the rest of the night on our hands and knees, wiping the floors at the facility with wet towels to get them clean. After sleep deprivation, we played the Synanon Game. All this was called therapy but I don't know where it came from. Some of it came from Synanon, and some of it more closely resembled POW brainwashing techniques. (It is interesting to note that the *Wall Street Journal* has a fairly recent story that the suspected Al Qaeda terrorists in Guantanamo Bay are being forced to stand in uncomfortable stress positions and are deprived of sleep, and there is some concern that international treaties banning torture of prisoners are being violated. These are the same techniques that were called therapy at Tarzana.)

And it's a good thing that the facility floors were clean from our all-night "cleaning parties" as sometimes therapy took a strange turn. One day we yellow phasers were standing on the wall, and Etta told us to turn around. A very long hall ran down the center of The Family section of the facility.

"Lay down on your bellies," Etta said. All ten yellow phasers got down on the floor and stretched out with our cheeks flat against the floor. Etta picked Billy and told him to slither down the hallway like a snake while making a hissing noise. Billy started pushing himself with his toes while he wiggled his upper torso. Pushing and wiggling, he slid a couple of hundred feet down the hall, hissing and sputtering as he went. Sweat began to form on his brow from the exertion, and dirt streaks marked the right side of his face. Then Etta tapped each one of us in turn on the shoulder and said, "Your turn." Soon there were ten human snakes, some with paper bags over their heads, sliding and squirming down the corridor, hissing all the way.

"All right," Etta said, "stop the hissing. Say, 'I'm a snake and I like it that way.'"

An ill-timed chorus of voices began to mumble, "I'm a snake and I like it that way" with background rustling, scratching noises as bodies undulated to and fro from one end of the hallway to the other. The mantra continued until lunchtime when we were allowed to get on our feet and walk to the cafeteria, magically transformed back into human beings again.

The Family at Tarzana wasn't the only program like this or even the worst. The Seed was another program. Straight Inc. was another that was formed a few years later and had numerous allegations of abuse leveled against it, including the use of "spit therapy." Spit therapy is spitting in someone's face and yelling at that person for an hour or so, supposedly to help them get honest. Etta James calls the therapy "abuse" in her book but also calls it one of the great adventures of her life.

Tarzana had an impact on me, no doubt, but I cannot honestly say that it gave me the tools to live life on life's terms. In other words, there was a sort of therapy but it was not sensible therapy. It was certainly not effective, humane, enlightened therapy.

Some of what happened to me at Tarzana was beneficial but other parts of the program definitely were not. It certainly was not beneficial to be verbally attacked and excited into a state of intense hatred. It added more trauma to my already severely traumatized life

However, to the extent that the verbal attacks contained some truth and broke though my denial, they were helpful. What was more helpful was that I saw people who had been drug addicts and who were now staying clean for a period of years; I had never known anyone like that, and it was novel and somewhat inspiring to me. An example is always the best kind of preaching.

I can't say that I was taught much about the nature of addiction or even the solution to my problem. Of course, the staff was not able to teach me what they didn't know. As far as my addiction, I was told by one of the elders of the program that I was "running from my feelings." There is an element of truth in that, but more about that later.

I stayed at Tarzana for about four months. It was a living hell.

For several years prior to entering Tarzana I had been experiencing debilitating migraine headaches behind my left eye, probably due to drug use or repressed emotions. When they hit I was in agony. One hit me while I was in Tarzana. The pain was unbearable. It was as if a pointed dagger had been thrust deep into my eye. The pain became so intense that tears flowed from the corner of my eye. In desperation, I asked to see a nurse. I walked into the room and the nurse asked me what was wrong.

"I'm having a horrible migraine headache," I told her.

"How long has it been hurting?"

"All day today, and half the day yesterday." I wiped a tear from my eye.

"We can't give you anything for it."

"You don't understand. It hurts. Real bad. My dad gets headaches like this too. It runs in my family."

I could see the suspicious look on her face. She thought I was gaming her. She picked up a chart and wrote on it. "It's psychosomatic," she said.

"I don't care if it's psychosomatic or not. It hurts just the same"

"I'm sorry. We can't give you anything for it. It's all in your head."

Resentfully, I left the room in pain.

Another day after running laps, I sat at the rear of the facility and cried. One of the candidates walked up to me and asked what was wrong. I looked up at him with tears running down my face. "I want to fix so bad I don't know what I'm going to do," I said. He nodded in understanding.

Some of the staff at Tarzana had familiarity with hypnosis and my falling into a trance had not gone unnoticed. Another time in a Synanon Game I started to get angry at what was being said to me. We were sitting in a circle with staff and residents surrounding us. My anger again made me susceptible to hypnotic suggestion. With seeming authority a paid staff member, told me, "There are too many of us here. You can't do anything. All you can do is sit in that chair and take it." I was mad.

"There is nothing you can do but sit there and take it. You're stuck in that chair. Go ahead and try. You can't get out of the chair. You can't," the staff member said.

I struggled and writhed to get out of the chair but I couldn't.

"The harder you try, the harder it gets to get out of the chair." Hypnotists call this the law of reversed effort, but I didn't know it at the time or even that I was in a waking hypnotic state.

I futilely struggled in frustration to get out of the chair. I was actually stuck in my chair and couldn't get out. Try as hard as I could, I just could not get out. I didn't understand what was happening.

Then suddenly the staff member switched directions and told me, "Hold onto that chair tightly because the wind is blowing, and it's blowing you out of the chair." I gripped the side of the chair, and my back arched as if a real wind was blowing me out of the chair. Then he told me, "The wind is dying down" and I slumped back into the chair as the imaginary wind died down. At that point staff members had determined I was highly suggestible, and prone to falling into trance states while under stress.

Someone must have made the decision to use my suggestibility and trance states to "solve" my drug problem. Because of my mental state at the time and because it was more than thirty years ago, I have a hard time recalling exactly what happened. My recollection is that I fell into a trance and they gave me a post-hypnotic suggestion that my heroin problem was gone. Did it really happen? I can't be sure. Maybe yes, maybe no. At any rate, what is clear is that I was highly suggestible and that they experimented on me using suggestion.

As my days at Tarzana neared an end, a new parole officer visited me and I got the sense from him that if I left, my parole would not be violated. My original motivation had been to keep from returning to prison and, when that threat receded, I no longer felt obligated to stay. Although I was experiencing some change, Tarzana was also a living hell as far as what we had to go through. So around dawn one morning I snuck out the back door with my shaved head. I was stopped at six a.m. by two cops in a police cruiser wondering what I was doing wandering the early morning streets. I must have looked like quite a sight with my shaved head. I explained to them that I had just left the psychiatric hospital. Their eyes widened and they asked me if I was okay now. I assured them I was. They did not arrest me as I had violated no laws.

This was the end of my stint in rehab. Thirty years later I'm still wondering what all these crazy therapies had to do with overcoming a drug problem.

Chapter 7

"Sympathy for the Devil"

After leaving Tarzana I stayed at a motel for a week. It was the lowest point of my life. I was contemplating suicide and even toying with razor blades on my wrists. Despite the post hypnotic suggestion, I still wanted drugs. Somehow I got hooked up with a fellow who said he could get heroin. I said I would do anything to get it.

While I stayed at the motel I ran into a "Christian" who started evangelizing me. In my apartment he asked me if I accepted Jesus Christ as my Savior. Tersely, I said yes. He waived his hand and told me I was saved, but I felt no real change. Several times he came over afterward but I would not answer the door for him. Whatever had happened it was not a life-changing experience but more the repeating of words under pressure.

I remembered a nearby church, and found my way there. When I entered the church, I found a very unusual scene. There were at least a hundred people in the church, and they were all kneeling in prayer, making unintelligible, meaningless noises. I found it very strange to say the least. It was not as strange as Tarzana, but weird in its own way. I sat down in a pew, but felt very out of place as everyone was babbling. Up at the front of the church was a large wooden cross, and some fellow was hugging the base of the cross and pounding on it while yelling out loudly in an emotional way, "Oh, Jesus." He kept yelling it out over and over. I knelt down in prayer in the pew to fit in. Everybody was babbling and I thought that's what I should be doing too, so I began babbling unintelligible noises to fit in. After a while I left that particular church and never returned.

I returned to my parents' house. In addition to the post-hypnotic suggestion implanted in me at Tarzana, I had, at long last, realized I had a drug problem. There are those who still promote hypnosis as the cure for addiction but it cannot work, as it doesn't resolve the root issues of why a person is using drugs in the first place.

It's amazing that someone could be on drugs for so long and sink as low as I had and not realize he has a problem, but that was the case. I had always felt that society had the problem by making drugs illegal. I became determined not to use illegal drugs. However, I could certainly drink, couldn't I? After all, it's legal.

Back at home I went to work in another restaurant during the graveyard shift. Shortly after I began working there, I was in the kitchen talking to the restaurant manager.

"Have you ever seen this?" he asked. He stood there holding his hands out in front of his stomach, clasped together in prayer like fashion. "Put your hands together like this," he said. "Push them together as hard as you can." He paused for a moment. "Keep pushing them together."

I did as I was told.

"Your hands are stuck together now," he announced. This is a hypnotic induction technique known as a "Coue Clasp."

I walked out to the front part of the kitchen. Then I tried to pull my hands apart. They were stuck fast together. I struggled to pull them apart, but they were still stuck. I walked back into the kitchen and told the manager my hands were stuck together.

He looked at me curiously and said in a loud voice, "You're going to work hard while you're here whether you like it or not." After a pause he told me, "You can take your hands apart now." Suddenly I was able to get my hands apart. And I did work hard for the year I was employed there. It seemed my fate to keep running into people familiar with mind control and hypnosis.

I was able to stay away from drugs for the first time in a long time. My old connection, Don, looked me up and tried to get me to use drugs. I refused.

Although I was not using illegal drugs, I did drink heavily and regularly on Friday and Saturday nights. A female neighbor with a bad drinking problem accompanied me to bars throughout the city. I basically substituted drinking for drug use.

After I quit the restaurant job, I became involved with a woman who had been at Synanon, which may have had something to do with my attraction to her. She was also very pretty. At any rate my relationship with her was not healthy. In fact, none of my relationships with women up to that time had been emotionally healthy. As they say in AA, two sickos don't make a wello. When the relationship broke up, I resorted to heavy drinking.

I lost my job, and ended up at the house of a homosexual friend of my former girlfriend. She had many homosexuals for friends. They had been constantly after me when I was dating her, but I did not have those inclinations. Depressed from the broken relationship, I had nowhere to stay and was invited into his home.

Somehow my dad found out where I was and came to see me. I'm sure he was concerned. He stood in the living room and said, "I want to talk to my son."

My hatred for him came out and I said, "You have no son anymore. Get the hell out of here." How that must have hurt him. I was deep in the grasp of evil and hate.

During one of my drunken sprees at the time, I called Tarzana and said I wanted to come back. They said I could. When asked when I was coming, I only answered, "Soon."

Shortly thereafter, I went to my parents' house. They were in the living room watching TV. I went into the bedroom, and put my mother's purse under my coat. Then I walked into the laundry room, and threw the purse out the window. Although I was stealing to get money for drugs, there was something more at work there that I didn't understand at the time, repressed rage playing itself out.

I drove to the connections house, and I remember going into the trunk of the car to get the money out of my mother's purse. I felt so very ashamed of myself. As a minister friend of mine likes to say, "We are ashamed by the Light of a power greater than ourselves." That Light was working in my life to some extent. My conscience was still alive and trying to redeem me.

I checked myself into the Tarzana detox shortly after that.

While in detox I received a visitor. She walked into the detox as I was lying in bed.

"Hi, Ted," she said. I looked at her and didn't recognize who she was.

It must have shown on my face. "You don't recognize me," she said with a frown.

I looked at her more intently, studying her face and searching my memory. All of a sudden it came to me.

"Caroline," I exclaimed. The last time I had seen her was in my first stay in Tarzana. She had split during yellow phase to help her kids. "You came back!"

"Yes," she said. "I came back after you left, and finished the program."

I was impressed.

"You were an elder!" I said.

She nodded and I could detect a hint of pride.

"I've been using," I said, "but I'm not strung out."

"Well, go back to sleep," she said. "I just wanted to drop by and say hello." She gave me a hug and then turned to walk out of the detox dorm. There were three or four other addicts there at the time, all engaged in conversation.

She stopped and addressed them all. "Would you guys keep it down? Somebody is trying to sleep."

It was an act of kindness. She had come to make me feel welcome, and show that she remembered and cared about me. It was an act of love that I didn't really appreciate at the time. God bless her.

I was put back into the candidacy, but my mental state was such that I was unable to stay. The prospects of the rigors of the Tarzana program were too much for me, and I again fled. Irving, my buddy and another graduate, followed me out the door and tried to stop me, but I would have none of it. As he called out my name, I turned my back and left. Caroline and Irving, and perhaps others, no doubt had concern for me. It was not my time, nor did anyone have the understanding to be able to help me. I left Tarzana never to return.

Although many of the people at Tarzana were well intentioned, the therapy (if you can call it that) did not really address a person's drug addiction. Nor could it ever—a tax-supported institution like Tarzana cannot, by law, be in the business of evangelism, even if they had the understanding to lead a person to tears of redemption. These days Tarzana appears to be in the twelve step business, but there are real problems with modern twelve step programs also.

After leaving Tarzana I turned myself into my parole officer. He told me my parents were not going to prosecute me for stealing the purse.

Amazingly, I was not violated, but my parole agent said he would have to write a report to the board, and they would decide what to do. While waiting for this to happen, I stayed at a skid row hotel and got drunk. While drunk I attempted a burglary of a dentist's office for drugs, and I was arrested again. My fourteen-year downward journey of crime and drugs had come to an end.

SECTION 2: UP
(The Journey Back Home)

Chapter 8

The Compassion of the Father

"But while he was still a long way off, his father saw him and was filled with compassion"[3]

After being arrested for this latest burglary, I appeared again at Torrance Superior Court. After nine years of appearing in and out of court, they basically were at a loss as to what to do with me, as they are with many people. What they did was recommit me for a second seven-year commitment to CRC.

My stay at CRC this time was a little over a year. During that time I started attending both Alcoholics Anonymous and Narcotics Anonymous meetings. I liked the Alcoholics Anonymous meetings more than the Narcotics Anonymous meetings, perhaps because of my negative experiences with drug addicts. At any rate I started attending the meetings weekly even though I was not required to do it.

My suffering had brought me to the point where I was open-minded and wanted answers (is this not the purpose of suffering?). Faithfully, I attended the meetings. At that time (1976)

---

[3]   Luke 15:20

some of the AA's who came into the institution had thirty-plus years of sobriety, which would have made them nearly AA pioneers. Some had very good things to say, and I know that a few really had the spiritual awakening that is talked about in the twelve steps. However, their contact with us inmates was limited to an hour. It is also true that many of the twelve-steppers who came in were just as lost as us inmates.

Narcotics Anonymous was still in its formative years, and had not yet gained widespread popularity. Very few of the people who came into the institution had significant amounts of "clean time." Nine years was the most I remember seeing. But at any rate I was open-minded, and attended the meetings.

I even attended church a few times while in the institution. Various churches and evangelists came into the institution, and I listened to a radio ministry. I was interested in these things— at that point I believe I was searching for the truth.

Perhaps one of the most important things the institution did for me was dry me out. A period of enforced sobriety gave my head some time to clear. This is another reason why drugs should remain illegal: we can force inmates to stay clean (if we can keep drugs out of the prisons) and this by itself has a real value. Of course, there were drugs at CRC while I was there, but they weren't plentiful.

When the time came for me to be paroled I had nowhere to go. My family was resentful and disillusioned with my prospects for recovery. How could they be anything else? I remember one of the parole board members deriding me with judgment and resentment: "You damn drug addicts, even your own families don't want you." And it was true. I made arrangements to go to a halfway house in Long Beach since there was nowhere else I could go to.

On April 1, 1977, I paroled out into the outside world. I had come to the realization that I had a drinking/drug problem, and I had been exposed to people who were no longer drinking or using drugs. I had even been exposed to some authentic spirituality.

When the prison bus dropped us off at the Norco bus stop, most of the parolees went into the liquor store for a beer and alcohol with their two hundred dollars in gate money. I had had enough AA that I was at least able to not do that.

However, it didn't last long, I was at a bar several days later. Not so much to drink, but seeking female companionship. There had been no teaching about sexuality in the institution except for a pornographic flick the institutional staff allowed in for inmate viewing. I don't know if the California Department of Corrections still allows pornographic films inside the institutions, but they certainly did in 1976.

I stayed in the bar for several hours while I drank ginger ale, but eventually I succumbed to the temptation to drink. The next thing I knew it was the morning after, and I was waking up at a motel, slightly hung over. And I was afraid. I was deathly afraid that I was never, ever going to be able to stop drinking—ever. And this meant I wouldn't be able to stop using drugs, for when I drank, I also used drugs. This is the state of my mind so accurately described in the *Big Book of Alcoholics Anonymous* as "no mental defense against the first drink" (or as the Scripture says, "For the good that I want, I do not do, but I practice the evil that I do not want[4]). I found that when I wanted to stop drinking I was unable to do so. I was powerless, and that is frightening.

---

[4]   Romans 7:19

At this time my sister offered to let me stay at her home. I left the halfway house and moved in with her. It was in Orange County, away from most of my drug connections. This was good for me, and protective of my very fragile early recovery. It was somewhat of a shield from the temptation of drugs. At least I did not have former connections coming to my house to try and get me to use or sell drugs.

I landed a job working at a branch of one of the restaurants where I had worked in Los Angeles. My experience at the bar had put enough fear in me that I started attending AA meetings on the outside too, not as a condition of my parole but voluntarily.

Alcoholics Anonymous

Although there were Narcotics Anonymous meetings in Los Angeles, they were few and far between in 1977. And, when I went to them, not many people were staying clean at that time. One of the few meetings I could find was at a "treatment center", and it was at least a half-hour drive away. When I went to the meeting, I found that there was nobody with more than a few months clean.

So I found a home at Alcoholics Anonymous, and began to find out what it was all about. I had experienced AA within the prison, and now I was about to experience it on the outside. At that time drug addicts with drinking problems were more or less tolerated in AA. There were some kind AA's who welcomed us, but there were others who clearly resented our presence there and said so.

First of all, let me start by saying that Alcoholics Anonymous does perform a service in our society. As someone who benefited somewhat from the existence of Alcoholics Anonymous, I do not want to appear as an ingrate. Nevertheless, I believe it is important to be truthful. Over thirty years I have attended many hundreds of meetings of both Alcoholics Anonymous and Narcotics Anonymous. The twelve steps the founders of Alcoholics Anonymous derived from the teachings of the Oxford Group (also known as First Century Christian Fellowship or Moral Rearmament) and the New Testament are true principles for the most part (with some exceptions). And it is also true that an authentic spiritual awakening is the solution to either an alcohol or drug problem.

However, my experience with both AA and NA is that the majority of people merely substitute their addiction to drugs or alcohol for an addiction to meetings, and the comforts and friendships they find there. This is not to say that I don't believe there are rare individuals here and there who actually do wake up from the psychic sleep they live in, but not many. If you are one of the many individuals who has benefited to some extent from these programs, I hope you will realize that my criticism of the programs is well-meaning. And perhaps you will see through some of these programs' institutionalized lies (i.e., you have a disease). It is the Truth that sets us free, not lies.

Amazingly, although I had attended AA meetings in the institution for over a year, I had not read the *Big Book of Alcoholics Anonymous*, which is the basis of the AA program. At that time the third edition of the *Big Book* was being used. Some of the ideas presented in that book are valid, but not all. The teaching about resentment and anger can be life saving if taken to heart and applied with sincerity, honesty, and grace.

I started attending Alcoholics Anonymous meetings regularly. I had an AA background from jail, and found meetings similar on the outside. As a matter of fact, some of the best AA meetings I ever attended were in prison. At any rate the meetings I attended in the institution were mainly speaker meetings, so I started regularly attending a speaker meeting in Orange, California. During one of the meetings, they asked for someone to be an intergroup representative. Nobody wanted to do it, so I volunteered. I had no idea what an intergroup representative did, but I had been told to be of service. I found out in Southern California each AA group had an intergroup representative, and they go to meetings of all the intergroup reps and discuss issues that effect AA as a whole.

At one of my first intergroup meetings, I witnessed the controversy that was wracking AA at the time: Should meetings for homosexuals be marked gay (G) in the meeting list? During the late 1970's homosexual activism was at its height. Homosexuals were clamoring for acceptance within society, and were also seeking acceptance within Alcoholics Anonymous. The AIDS epidemic had not yet reared its head. Many of the intergroup representatives were adamant in their opposition to the proposal. I remember one lady walked off in disgust, shaking her head to and fro. In the end the proposal was sold to the crowd on the basis of "If you know which meetings are gay, then you know which ones to avoid." That was the nose of the camel in the tent, so to speak.

I began to be more and more steeped in the culture of Alcoholics Anonymous. After serving as an intergroup representative, I was elected secretary of the speaker meeting. I handled the donations and bought birthday cakes, but the responsibility for getting speakers was left to someone else. For me the Saturday night speaker meeting was an important part of my early recovery. I heard many interesting stories, and while at meetings I stayed out of trouble. Some of the old-timers there had been coming for more than thirty years which means they were early AA pioneers.

I distinctly remember one man I call one-armed Charlie. He had been an AA member for more than thirty years, and regularly attended the meeting. I asked Les (the person who procured the speakers) why they never had him speak since he had been sober for so long. Les got a strange look on his face that I didn't understand at the time. Apparently my comments had some impact. Several weeks later, Charlie was a speaker. His story was interesting, but not particularly impressive. I remember him telling how he won two lotteries when he decided to get sober. It sounded slightly improbable, but I had heard many improbable stories in AA. I gave it little thought.

I served out my remaining time as secretary of the meeting, and then relinquished it to someone else.

Some afternoons I hung out at the AA club; I was becoming an AA regular. After a few months I noticed that one-armed Charlie was no longer around the club. I asked someone, "Hey, where is Charlie?" That's when it was explained to me that Charlie had been involved sexually with some of the younger women in Alcoholics Anonymous in a way one would not want advertised in a newspaper, and had ended up killing himself with a bullet to the brain.

Despite the somewhat rude awakening with Charlie, I continued to go to AA meetings. I usually went two or three times a week. I was able to stay sober five years, which was quite an accomplishment for me— something I had not done for a decade and a half.

I did have an "awakening" at this time, and it was frightening. One day while working on my new job as a pest control operator in a vacant house, I noticed a prescription pill vial on the countertop. I became fixated and fascinated with the pill vial, and felt myself drawn to it. I was being tempted to take the drugs. At the same time I felt something mysterious happening to me. I sensed something eerie and evil— I felt myself being "absorbed" is the best way I can describe it. The moment of temptation passed, and I did not fully understand what had transpired.

The next day I called the pastor who had been trying to help me, and explained to him what had happened. He explained to me that I had sensed and discerned in a spiritual way something evil inside of me. He explained when you see a tree it's because the light is illuminating it, and that we don't notice the light that reveals it so much. Discernment by an inner light is similar. He explained to me that it had gotten inside me through my use of drugs. He also explained that I needed to continue in prayer and meditation, and that it would come out of me.

It is an understatement to say I was terrified. I had not believed in the existence of evil, but now I discovered that not only did it exist, but also that it existed inside of me! It was horrifying to realize this and scary beyond belief. I locked myself in my apartment for weeks on end while I did little more than pray and meditate. Whom could I talk to about it? The minister recommended I not go to AA meetings for a while, saying the people there might be more of a hindrance than a help.

Suddenly one morning I experienced a horrifying pain in my chest like a heart attack. I felt like I was dying. I tumbled out of bed, and got down on my knees and cried out to God, saying I would never doubt him again. The pain in my chest stopped and my head jerked and I felt something come out of me. I was elated. I ran downstairs, passed the manager of the apartment building, and exclaimed, "Today is the best day of my life!" However, my newfound happiness was to be short lived.

A woman entered the picture, but I do not want to blame her. It was my own weakness and failing that led to my undoing. The woman was my old girlfriend, Cindy, who had looked me up. One thing led to another, and I was involved in sexual sin. Worse, although she was separated from her husband and in the process of getting a divorce, she was still married. I had broken the commandment to not covet my neighbor's wife. My conscience, however, had become more developed through abstinence from alcohol, and I was terribly conscience stricken about the whole affair. I felt like I had kicked God in the teeth. I called up my minister friend and told him that. He said that was exactly what I had done.

My concern was that I had committed the unforgiveable sin. I asked my minister if there was forgiveness for someone like me.

His answer: "I think there is, but I'm not God. Why don't you just start living a decent life?"

I ended up marrying Cindy, but I realized I did not have love and had been selfish and used her. Like all marriages that start on the wrong foot, our marriage was definitely not a match made in heaven. How can any woman respect a man who ignores principle in favor of sex before marriage? That's not a popular point of view in our modern age, but it is true nonetheless. Within a few short months, we were at each other's throats, and she soon left me. I was resentful at her as well as my mother-in-law for her meddling.

I soon found myself in a bar drunk again. This was my five-year "slip."

As you can see, my path to permanent sobriety and peace of mind involved some very long detours. A long, long period of recovery and rehabilitation lay ahead of me with a seemingly endless series of realizations.

Although I was off drugs and alcohol, I was sadly lacking in the skills to succeed in life. I had gone back to school to learn to be a welder, so I could find employment other than as a short-order cook in restaurants. At night I worked as a cook during the graveyard shift, and in the morning I attended welding school. After a few semesters I gained employable skills, but was by no means a truly competent welder. I landed a job as a welder at a company that made sheet metal cabinets, which required only minimal skills. I worked there for several years.

My sobriety continued. My involvement with Alcoholics Anonymous continued, but to a lesser extent. And my interest in Christianity continued and increased. After several years I began to think more clearly.

As a result of my interest in Christianity, I also became interested in the pro-life movement. I became convinced of the horrible injustice that was occurring to the unborn child as well as my personal obligation as an aspiring Christian to do something. Graphic photos of mangled aborted fetuses convinced me I had to do something. In 1984 I put a small ad in a Christian magazine asking for help in picketing our local federal courthouse. A group of six or so of us began to picket at the federal courthouse in Los Angeles. After a while we decided to take our picketing to the local abortion clinic. We discovered during our picketing that sometimes we could persuade women or couples going into the clinic to keep their babies, and babies began to be saved on a regular basis. We began to counsel at another clinic across town without the picket signs, and babies were also saved. Thus began one of the most life-changing experiences for me, and for others too I believe.

We found a third clinic in Rosemead, and we began to counsel at the clinic every Sunday morning. Almost every Sunday a small group of two to eight of us did sidewalk counseling in front of the clinic. And almost every Sunday women and couples kept a baby or two, sometimes as many as five.

Standing up for what was right was therapy for me. Instead of being a hopelessly addicted alcoholic, drug addict, burglar, and abuser of my fellow man, I was doing something worthwhile. It is true that at times I was egotistical about what I was doing, but it is also true that it was a far cry from being a dope dealer and a pharmacy burglar.

My very active pro-life involvement continued throughout the 1980's. Most of the people in the pro-life movement were unaware of my sordid past at that time. And, of course, I had nothing to do with any of the violence that occurred at abortion clinics during that time.

So standing up against injustice became a life-changing therapy for me. It was one of the most satisfying times of my life. I was getting better.

Chapter 9

Persecuted For Righteousness Sake

"Blessed are they which are persecuted for righteousness' sake: for theirs is the kingdom of heaven."(Matthew 5:10)

I held a steady job as a welder and did counseling on the weekends. I had become stable. My attendance at Alcoholics Anonymous meetings began to wane. Sometimes it would be months between meetings. However, I felt secure in my sobriety, and had realized my well-being depended on my relationship with God, not on any attendance at meetings. And I discovered that when I was trying to do what was right in God's eyes that doors opened for me.

One of the sidewalk counselors at the abortion clinic, a man named Bart, was also a real estate appraiser, and he offered the opportunity to any of us counselors to learn the appraisal profession. I was interested, and began to ride along with him to learn. However, I could only do it on weekends due to my other job. It would have taken a long time to learn at that rate, but my situation changed when my employer started laying off people based on seniority. I had just enough seniority to avoid the cut, but it seemed like the perfect opportunity to me. I volunteered to be laid off; it allowed someone else to keep his job. I was able to collect unemployment while I learned a new trade. At age 36 I began to learn a new profession. It was an opportunity that came to me from the most unexpected source. It was an unforeseen blessing— God's reward to me for standing up for what was right.

For the next five years, I continued to do sidewalk counseling and pursue the appraisal profession. My appraisal friend moved to another state, and I continued to work for his partner. After several years I realized he was extremely selfish, often taking the lion's share of the fees we earned. It meant opportunities for me would be limited. I decided to transfer my appraisal skills to real estate sales, and went to school to get my real estate license.

During the classes they addressed the issue of whether someone with a criminal record could get a license. I was told if I revealed my arrest history that I would not be denied a license. So I finished my classes, took the necessary tests, and applied for a license. The California Licensing Authority processed my application, but they took a very long time to do it. This was 1986; my last arrest had been a decade earlier. I was able to provide numerous character reference letters from the pro-life people who had come to know me.

After a wait of many months, I contacted the licensing people. They were reluctant to issue a license due to my record. The woman with whom I was dealing said they would issue a probationary license. Of course, I objected to that. What broker would want a salesperson with a probationary license? Reluctantly, the state issued me a real estate salesperson license. My criminal record would continue to haunt me for the next twenty-five years.

Thus I began a new career as a real estate salesperson. I had some early success as I began to learn about the real estate world. I discovered that many of the agents in real estate are a greedy, unprincipled lot. Not all of course, but far too many. To a large degree, it was a world of backstabbing and betrayal. During my training the trainer at the company even advised me not to do anything illegal unless "it was really profitable."

During this time I continued doing appraisal work part-time, but my main focus was real estate sales. It was 1988 and the real estate market in the San Gabriel Valley area was hot. I put in long, long hours trying to make a success of myself, but I discovered that becoming a successful real estate agent is not easy. In the San Gabriel Valley many of the buyers were Chinese, and preferred to work with Chinese agents only. And I also discovered that sellers were more interested in having experienced agents. The number of agents in the Valley was staggering; there were too many deer in the forest, but I gave it a good old college try. For three years I eked out a living, and learned quite a bit about real estate and the greedy cutthroat business world— the world of drugs addicts is not the only world of sin. I also continued my sidewalk counseling activities.

During this time I was also questioning of some of the things I had been taught in Alcoholics Anonymous: such as "once an alcoholic always an alcoholic," and that we are "like men who have lost their legs, we never grow new ones." However, my pastor had said that a person could drink in moderation after having a "spiritual awakening." It had been close to eight years since I had last gotten drunk. I felt I had had a spiritual awakening. I was determined to give myself a test.

One day at lunch I ordered a beer to go with my sandwich. I had not drunk alcohol in so long that the solitary glass of beer made me woozy, and a little light-headed. I have to say I didn't even like the feeling anymore. I liked being aware. The drink made me less aware, and I didn't like that. I truly was changed. And that was all that happened. No mysterious craving kicked in as I had been taught would happen in AA. Over the next several years, I tried this experiment several more times with the same result. I was free!

Of course, I realize all this flies in the face of what is taught about alcoholism and drug addiction in general. Those steeped in the AA culture will immediately say that I really wasn't an alcoholic. However, I had attended hundreds if not thousands of meetings and had easily identified myself as being a "low bottom" drunk as well as a drug addict. I had taken the famous twenty questions of AA, and answered nineteen of them in the affirmative. Others may say that I have not remained sober, but I know in my heart that is not the truth. My ability to control my drinking was restored— I had no desire to do it anymore, and certainly no desire to drink in excess.

My drinking experiment was just that: an experiment. In subsequent years I rarely drank at all. On a rare occasion I might have a couple of ounces of wine before bedtime for its beneficial effect on my heart and to lower cholesterol. I never returned to abusive drinking or even drinking on a regular basis. A few alcohol researchers are beginning to realize the truth that a heavy drinker or "alcoholic" can be restored to a state of self-control where he can safely drink temperately.[5] Of course, all this flies in the face of what the modern recovery movement is teaching about alcoholism, but the sad truth is that we live in the dark ages of both alcoholism and drug addiction treatment. The very experts in charge of treating alcoholics don't even understand it themselves. They falsely believe and teach that the alcoholic has a disease, and is somehow different bodily from other people. That is all complete nonsense.

---

[5]   Hebert Fingarette, *Heavy Drinking—The myth of Alcoholism as a Disease.*

I want it to be clear that I am not advocating that those in early recovery go out and drink. Indeed, for those who have not truly resolved their underlying issues it could be exceedingly dangerous. Also, I want to add that I have no problem with those who prefer complete abstinence from alcohol due to their bad experiences. But I want to be truthful and state that for those who have had an authentic spiritual awakening, there is no danger in a drink in moderation. Again, not a popular point of view, but true nevertheless.

At about this time the Operation Rescue movement (OR) was sweeping the country, including Los Angeles. Although we had been sidewalk counseling for about four years, we had stayed within the limits of the law except for minor trespassing on the clinic parking lot. We had discussed civil disobedience, but had refrained from doing any. That was about to change. Randall Terry, Joseph Foreman, and others had been engaging in successful massive sit-ins on the East Coast, and they brought their message of massive non-violent sit-ins to Los Angeles. Some of the churches in Los Angeles supported OR; some did not. It was an exhilarating time.

The first few protests were successful in closing clinics without arrests. One memorable moment was the Los Angeles police asking OR leaders to leave peacefully because people would die in emergency situations in other parts of the city if they had to bring in officers to arrest everybody. OR leadership responded by saying people would die at the clinic if they left. It was an impasse. The Los Angeles police were reluctant to make large arrests at first, but that changed.

One morning the caravan of OR cars assembled, and the leaders drove to the target clinic. In a few minutes OR people had "taken the door" (positioned the first sit-in protestors). Pro-abortion demonstrators (mainly radical feminists and people from the gay rights movement) closed in quickly. Although the pro-abortion people have always denied it, many assaults against peaceful protestors took place at this time. Eventually at least a thousand or so pro-life demonstrators successfully positioned themselves to blockade the clinic entrances.

The first arrests started to take place. Unfortunately, Los Angeles Police Department officials decided to use pain compliance against the peaceful demonstrators. Operation Rescue took the position that they don't walk away from the scene of murders, and asked the police to carry off the demonstrators on stretchers to prolong the protest (this had been done in other places). They refused. Instead they applied pain compliance holds on the demonstrators. This involved using martial arts nunchuks to inflict pain on the demonstrators, so they would get up and walk to the waiting buses. Personally, I thought both OR and the police were wrong. I thought OR could walk away slowly, and nothing was gained by forcing the police to use pain compliance. And I thought the police were wrong for using the pain compliance, especially on women. When my turn to be arrested came they asked me (as they did everyone) if I would get up and walk to the bus. Although everyone else forced the police to use pain compliance, I did not. I walked to the bus. It was considered a sign of cowardice by some of the pro-life protestors, but I just didn't see the point in getting hurt and accomplishing nothing.

I had several arrests at various Operation Rescue demonstrations, and they were deeply moving experiences. At the first arrest I remember looking out the window of the prisoner bus taking us away, and seeing tears stream down the face of a lady watching us being arrested. She was moved by the injustice of it all. For the most part judicial penalties meted out against the protestors were minimal. There was, however, some "sidewalk justice" applied by the police; like the dragging of Operation Rescue co-founder Joseph Foreman through horse feces left by the mounted police.

Operation Rescue leader Randall Terry pled not-guilty and went to trial with several other leaders. I don't think anybody really expected them to win, but they did. Apparently, enough evidence got to the jury about what was going on in the clinic, or they were so outraged at how the demonstrators were treated by the pain compliance that they acquitted the leadership.

Although we were offered deals of just minimal token fines, many of us refused to plead guilty. I went to trial with six other defendants for unlawful assembly and trespass. I was quite familiar with the court system due to all my drug arrests. When I was a criminal, the court system was quite scrupulous in protecting my rights. In fact, I beat a possession charge one time when I was guilty due to their failure to give me a speedy trial. But the one time I was innocent (innocent of any wrongdoing but technically guilty of trespass), the court was not so fair-minded.

The City Attorney's office had learned its lesson in the acquittal of Randall Terry and the other leadership, so they made sure we were not able to get a fair trial. They made legal motions to prohibit all the defendants from using words that had any pro-life connotation, and they forbade us from telling the jurors anything of what was happening inside the clinic. And, in the end, we all went to jail. The sentence was thirty days.

Of course, I was no stranger to the Los Angeles County Jail. But it was an entirely different experience to be in jail for a righteous cause instead of burglary charges. And I was in for some surprises. The Los Angeles Sheriff's Department personnel were not too happy overall in putting the Operation Rescue protestors in jail. The lieutenant in charge of the jail shift at the time we were processed called us all into his office. He was a Christian. He asked us to close the door, and then he prayed out loud for us for the heavenly Father to protect us during our stay. He also said he would arrange for us to be released on work release-type programs. However, it didn't happen for me. The lieutenant had anticipated that since we were involved in this type of activity that we had no police records. I was told he was shocked when he saw my arrest record, and so he couldn't approve any work release for me. My past continued to haunt me like a long shadow, even with another believer.

My thirty days in jail passed quickly. However, there was a flu circulating in the jail, and I caught it and was sick for quite some time. I found out standing up for what is right is not always without a price.

After I was released from jail, I could no longer do sidewalk counseling due to probation terms that did not allow us access within a certain distance of the clinic. And I was burned out to some extent after five years of counseling. My days of sidewalk counseling were done, at least for a while. I was also sentenced to two hundred hours of community service, which involved working for the city park service's trash detail. Once or twice a week I would arrive in the morning and drive around in a truck with a park employee, taking the trash-filled plastic bags out of the galvanized trashcans and putting in new plastic bags.

I finished my community service without incident. My real estate career was going nowhere, and I was just barely eking out a living. With my appraisal opportunities limited in Southern California and the recent Rodney King riots in Los Angeles, I decided to go to Oregon to work under my appraisal friend there.

Chapter 10

God Moves In Mysterious Ways

"God moves in a mysterious way His wonders to perform"—William Cowper

At this time however, due to the savings and loan scandal, the appraisal profession was starting to require licensing. I decided to go to Oregon, and apply for a license. I drove to Salem, Oregon, from Los Angeles, and took the tests and passed. My appraisal friend, Bart, was kind enough to let me stay at his house while I looked for housing.

However, something unexpected happened. My appraisal license was not issued.

Not only was it not issued, but I was not told the reason why. When I contacted the licensing board, they would not give me a reason but told me that my application was "under review." They did, however, issue me an assistant's license, which allowed me to work under the supervision of a licensed appraiser such as my friend. Of course, this was not the ideal situation, but it was doable.

After approximately four months my license had not been issued, and I was not being told the reason why. Finally, I decided to take action. I filed suit under the Americans with Disabilities Act alleging discrimination due to a disability (drug addiction), and made a complaint with the Equal Opportunity Employment Commission. I felt that I was being discriminated against. I felt that I had proved rehabilitation by more than fifteen years of good behavior, being drug free, and even holding a California Salesperson License without incident. My license had not been denied. They just didn't issue it, and wouldn't give me an explanation. Immediately after the lawsuit was served on the administrator, he responded by denying my license. It was clearly a case of retaliation against me for filing suit, which is illegal under the Americans with Disabilities Act. I responded by amending my suit alleging retaliation.

The second thing I did was make arrangements to testify against the citizen board that had to ratify the administrator's decision. Bart accompanied me to Salem for the hearing.

After the eight-member board took care of some routine business, the public was given an opportunity to comment. I sat in the chair, and began to speak from my heart. I was surprised to find myself getting choked up and emotional; I had to pause for a half-minute or so to regain my composure. Although not planned, I'm sure my distraught emotional state helped invoke some sympathy. I briefly told them my history, and how hard I had worked to become an appraiser. After I finished, Bart also testified to the board, giving me a glowing personal reference including my sidewalk counseling activities.

At the end the board voted to ratify the administrator's decision, and deny my license. The thing about drug use and rehabilitation is that it affects many, many people. As could be expected, some of the board members had family affected by drug use. Feelings were very high and strong on the issue. One board member yelled no at the top of his voice that he did not support the administrator's decision. When the final tally was taken, the vote was six to three against me. After the vote one of the board members let me know he had a recovered alcoholic in his family and that he was all for me.

Strangely enough, they did not revoke my assistant's license despite denying me a license and so I continued to work.

I was representing myself in federal court, and several people advised me to get an attorney. However, I was comfortable representing myself. Who could better represent me? After all, I had lived it, and who could be more passionate about my case than me?

At the next federal court hearing, I explained to the judge that all I wanted was to work. Federal court judges often deal with criminal drug addicts in the course of their everyday work, and they are quite familiar with the problem. This particular judge (a magistrate actually) had been a U.S. attorney, and was even more familiar with drug prosecutions. I don't think they see truly rehabilitated drug addicts all that often, so he was sympathetic to my cause.

God works in mysterious ways. During my real estate sales career, I had teamed up with a part-time real estate agent named Maya. It turned out her regular job was as a U.S. District Court judge's secretary in Los Angeles. And during that time I had told her about my past. After my OR experience I did a series of television programs about the drug problem on community access television, and showed her one of the shows. She was impressed— so much so that she had written me a letter of reference to the appraisal board testifying to my rehabilitation. Having a letter from a U.S. District Court judge's secretary had a very positive influence on this magistrate I am sure; it was something I never could have planned. And I thank God He let it happen.

As it turned out the reason for my license being denied was not what I had thought. When the legislature created the licensing board, they neglected to give it criminal record-checking authority. The administrator had not been able to confirm that I had told him the truth about my arrest history. Also he had not wanted me or the public to know the board did not have the authority to check criminal records. Their fear was that if this became common knowledge that applicants would lie on their applications. So he was stalling me while they worked on getting the state legislature to correct the problem. Perhaps I wouldn't have sued if I had known that.

The judge discerned that the problem was not my record. He made the comment that I only needed a couple more votes from the board. The judge himself had all the resources and authority necessary to get my entire criminal record. He asked me if it was okay with me if he gave the board a copy of my record. Of course, I didn't object since I had already given them the complete and truthful information, so the judge released the information to the administrator. He also applied pressure on the board by telling the state's attorney that he wanted them to reconsider my case based on the same information.

As luck (if you believe in luck) would have it, the attorney for the state was a nice young woman who could see the injustice of what was happening. She worked behind the scenes on my behalf, and lobbied board members to change their votes. I again appeared at a meeting of the board, and testified as to why I should be granted a license. This time the board was more sympathetic, and voted in my favor to give me a license. I had won. I was elated.

Chapter 11

Oregon

And so I settled down to a new life in Oregon as a real estate appraiser. I did attend church while in Oregon. I also attended meetings of Narcotics Anonymous and Alcoholics Anonymous. It was not so much for myself anymore, but to be of assistance to others. There were no abortion clinics in the part of Oregon where I lived, so sidewalk counseling was not an option.

I found Alcoholics Anonymous in Oregon to be very similar to Alcoholics Anonymous in Los Angeles, but there was less clapping at the meetings. I also attended meetings of Narcotics Anonymous which was something I had not really done since 1977. Sixteen years had passed since my release from prison, and Narcotics Anonymous had sort of grown up.

I kept my involvement with Narcotics Anonymous to a minimum of about once a week. I felt I should go considering my past. Although I did not agree with some of the program's principles, I thought I had something to offer. Most notably I could never accept the notion that alcoholism or drug addiction was a disease—it just flew in the face of common sense even though it is becoming such an accepted idea in our society. However, my belief was I could be helpful by going to the meetings and talking about some of the spiritual principles I had learned.

Of course, I never could say that I had experimented to see if I was able to drink in moderation. Such a truth is unacceptable within Narcotics Anonymous and Alcoholics Anonymous. Any drinking on my part during my years in Oregon (1992-2004) was minimal. Sometimes several years would pass before I would have a small glass of wine. It has been repeatedly proven to me that I didn't have anything to fear from a drink in moderation, but I preferred not to do it for the most part. Of course, I had stayed away from all drugs since my release from prison in 1977.

Some might consider my involvement in AA and NA hypocritical, but I don't. I knew my problem was solved, and thought I could be of assistance to others. Let me repeat what I have said before: don't get me wrong— I think in early recovery complete abstinence is wise. But at some point in recovery, a person can be so restored to sanity that he no longer has anything to fear from a drink in moderation. Of course this is unacceptable truth to the recovery movement in America, but it is true nonetheless.

Occasionally after meetings I would go to coffee or otherwise interact with others. There was a lady named Emilia who was a long-time member of Narcotics Anonymous. She was also a counselor at the local VA hospital's drug program. One day I went to her house for reasons I cannot remember; possibly, after a meeting, because she needed a ride. At any rate I drove up to her house, and we got out of the car. She went over to her mailbox, and got a letter out of the mailbox. She opened it and got a smile on her face.

"My viral count is down. My interferon is working," she said.

I was puzzled. I told her I didn't know what she was talking about.

"I've got hepatitis C," she said.

I vaguely knew that hepatitis was something you could catch from shooting drugs, but I knew very little about it. I told her so.

"It's rampant in the NA fellowship," she said.

"Well," I said, "I'm lucky I don't have it or worse. The way we used to shoot drugs and share needles it's a wonder I didn't catch anything. I'm lucky AIDS didn't exist when I was shooting drugs, or I would be dead for sure."

That was the end of the conversation, and I pitied the woman a little. I knew she had brought it on herself. I was glad I didn't have a disease like that.

I worked for my employer in southern Oregon. His company was expanding, and he had established branches in Roseburg and Portland. I was called on to manage his office in Portland, so I moved to Beaverton.

As anyone can tell you who has done it, it is a lonely experience to move to a city where you know absolutely no one. Fortunately, AA is everywhere, and I found myself frequenting an AA club in Beaverton which was a benefit to me. If you are in AA, you never have to be alone no matter where you live.

Two of the appraisal employees in our Portland office quit, and started their own appraisal company next door. Since we no longer had adequate staff, our major client began placing orders with them, and our business dwindled. Once again, the unexpected happened. Bart frequently worked long hours, and drove when he was tired. His wife was constantly reminding him of the danger, but to no avail. Exactly what happened that morning is not clear as Bart has no memory of it. He was driving down a two-lane country road, and apparently fell asleep at the wheel. He was involved in a head-on traffic collision.

Fortunately, no one was killed, but Bart broke his neck. A woman in the other car was seriously hurt. This threw the business into a worse uproar. Since the business was dwindling in Portland, he decided to close that office. James, the office manager running the business while Bart recuperated from his broken neck, decided to open a Eugene office. It was closer to the main office, and hence their supervision. There was still some business in Portland, and I was not inclined to move to Eugene. When the office closed I began doing appraisals out of my apartment, and my assistant in Portland was put in charge of the new Eugene office. I believe Bart and James were disappointed that I refused to go to Eugene, but I had to do what was right for me.

I can't remember how it all came about, but I ended up leaving Portland and returning to work at the main office in southern Oregon. There were five appraisers working in a small office. The office manager had his favorites, and there was resentment on the part of some of the appraisers over how they were treated. As the Eugene office started to prosper, it looked like a good opportunity to work there. I volunteered to go there, but was turned down because I didn't go when they wanted me to. I did not particularly like working there, and I saw no opportunity for advancement as long as the office manager was there.

As work began to slow down, one of Bart's clients called him and said they wanted to reduce fees significantly. Bart did not want to reduce fees, and thought that the client would have no choice but to pay the higher fees. I saw an opportunity, and took it. I called the client, and told them I was willing to work for the reduced fees. They agreed to send the work, and I started my own business. I felt justified at the time due to some of the treatment I had received previously. However, several years later I realized I had not treated

Bart right due to my ambition, and I was ashamed of myself. I later went to him and apologized.

Starting your own business is somewhat scary. I wasn't at all sure that the one client who was going to send me work was enough to live on. Sometimes the work was a long distance away, several hundred miles. But I was in no position to turn down any work, and that is how my business started. It slowly prospered. I found that good service was appreciated, and rewarded by clients. And then another woman came into my life.

Chapter 12

Judgment

"Judge not least ye be judged"—Matthew 7:1

I had continued my involvement in AA and NA. One day after a meeting in a recovery house, I met a woman named Diane. After the meeting we had coffee. Diane was newly off drugs, only a matter of weeks. In Alcoholics Anonymous and Narcotics Anonymous, "Thirteenth Stepping" abounds. Thirteenth Stepping is when someone with time (more than a year) decides to "date" a newcomer (someone with less than a year)— traditionally the AA program frowns on this type of behavior. I had never done it, and even had spoken against it at times.

If there is such a thing, Diane was not your typical drug addict in Narcotics Anonymous. She was not a user of illegal drugs as most NA's are. She was a nurse who had gotten hooked on Demerol as a result of her access to drugs in nursing. She had been in at least five different drug treatment programs, but none had been successful. I had good intentions with her from the beginning, but good intentions were not enough.

There was something operating below the level of my conscious mind, a programming I didn't understand at the time. It is called "trauma attraction." Let me try and explain this as I do not think it

97

is generally very well understood. I do know there are some good therapists and ministers who understand these things, but I'm afraid they are few and far between. When one is severely traumatized, the elements in the trauma scene produce either an attraction or revulsion. In my case the early childhood trauma with my mother caused me to be attracted to the elements in the trauma scene and what was in the trauma scene: a wrong woman, my mother. So my attraction to Diane was not sexual nor based on love although I did not understand it at the time. It was traumatic conditioning attracting me to a wrong woman like the mother who had beaten me as a child.

I did not understand this as it was happening. I experienced it only as attraction, and I thought it was "normal" attraction. I had been attracted to other women in the past who looked similar to my mother, but I equated it with normal attraction at that time also.

I had no love for Diane, although I thought I did. In other words, I was living in the delusion or illusion that I loved her. We became engaged, and we stayed engaged for two years. Diane was able to stay off drugs by hanging around with me. However, I crossed a moral border in the relationship with her. Frequently at night we would lie on the couch and engage in passionate French kissing. I did not consummate the sex act, but passionate kissing was certainly beyond the boundaries of what was right and proper. And crossing moral boundaries has an effect. I became addicted to her charms as much as I had ever been addicted to any drug. And I called this addiction "love."

Despite my protestations of love, women know when they are being used and when they are being loved. Diane certainly did. After several years she began seeing someone secretly on the side. Our engagement had ended sometime before, but I did not know she was seeing somebody. One day she broke the news to me.

It was incredible painful to me. My feelings were hurt. It had all been a big surprise to me. Unbeknownst to me, Diane had started seeing a Christian psychiatrist at an Overcomers Anonymous meeting at a local church. Diane and I had attended the meeting, and I felt betrayed. I was resentful.

Resentment had been the sin in my childhood that corrupted me originally. It was the negative thread weaved throughout my life. I seemed incapable of giving it up. Although I had been well schooled in the dangers of resentment in AA and at church, I was resentful nonetheless.

I had a hard time with this particular resentment. I knew the resentment was wrong yet I could not get over it. I experienced the depression that goes along with resentment.

I sought out counseling from a minister. He pointed out something to me that I had not realized. While it was true I hated the man who had "stolen" my girlfriend, there was also something else going on. Although I experienced it as hatred toward the person, there was also another more subtle resentment involved. I had difficulty recognizing it since it was like a big ball of resentment inside me. It was resentment toward my conscience for showing me I was wrong. Conscience is the place where God speaks to all of us who still have a conscience. And resentment of conscience is tantamount to hating God.

I was left with the stark realization that I hated God. It was embarrassing. But somehow I was also glad to realize it. At least I knew what was wrong. Simply stated, I was judging like a God, and hating the real God for showing me I was wrong for doing it. Being able to realize it somehow caused me to get over the resentment.

Also, about this time I started seeing through my own self-deception. I had honestly thought I loved Diane but after she left and I was no longer using her for my ego pleasure the truth began to dawn on me. One day on the road to Lakeview to do a job, I rounded a corner of the highway in my car, and all of a sudden I felt a deep rumbling within. The Truth dawned on me just how selfish I had been. My illusions were shattered. The pain was incredible, and I felt like I was dying. The spiritual pain was as painful as the broken arm I had had as a child. Without words something showed me just how selfish I was. Strangely, after the pain of the initial realization, I was left with an unfamiliar sadness and inner peace.

During this time of resentment toward the Christian psychiatrist, something else happened to me. One morning I was sitting in my apartment and I got up to walk across the room. I experienced a horrific pain in my chest like I had just been stabbed with a stiletto. I also felt like I was being pulled out of my body at the same time. I did the only thing I could do, which was to cry out to God to help me. Then suddenly I was back in my body lying on the floor. After lying there for a minute or so, I was able to get up. At first I thought it was indigestion. But I began to realize I had had a heart attack, and a fairly serious one at that. I sought out a doctor and got treatment.

The treatment I chose is something called chelation, which I had heard about but which is not generally accepted by the medical profession (at least a large segment of it). Thankfully, I have been able to avoid heart bypass surgery so far. I cannot prove it by any scientific means, but I know for sure that the heart attack was connected to my resentment. I began to more deeply understand the meaning of the scripture "Judge not lest ye be judged." My heart had been filled with hate, so is it any wonder I ended up with heart problems? I had learned a lesson about judging.

Somewhere around this period of time the long repressed resentment toward my mother started surfacing from my subconscious. I had thought I had forgiven her but I hadn't. The same minister who had shown me I had been hating God also advised me to speak to my mother about what she had done to me. So one day I went to her house. I had previously tried to confront her with the abuse but her attitude was denial at that time.

My father was alive at this time, but he was not home when the confrontation occurred. My mom was sitting in a chair in the living room.

"I need to talk to you," I said. "You can call it whatever you want, but the punishment you inflicted on me as a child was abuse. There's just no other word for it." As I spoke to her, feelings of resentment starting coming to the surface while I talked. It was like a long dormant vapor rising up inside me.

The confrontation with my mom caused tears to start streaming down her eyes. "There were lots of moms that were better moms than me. Lots of them," she said. She was crying profusely. "I hope this is not the reason you were on drugs."

Then she asked, "Why do you only remember the bad that happened and not the good?"

Speaking to her was surprising, disturbing, and uncomfortable for me.

About this time my father contracted colon cancer. Near the end I took off work, and drove down to California from Oregon. He was seated in the living room looking out the living room window when I approached him. He had suffered as much as I had during my years of addiction and criminality. He was looking emaciated now, almost like a skeleton. I knew the end was coming soon.

"Dad, I'm sorry I was such a bad son," I said, and then I gave him a hug. He started to cry.

Before I left I tried to talk to him about Christ. He would have none of it. He told me, "It would be hypocritical of me to believe now at the end."

I returned to Oregon. Several weeks later I got a call that my mom had found him lying on the garage floor. He went into the hospital, but was never released. He never really regained consciousness except for some brief moments, and I was never able to say much more to him.

Chapter 13

If Two Of You Agree On Earth
As Touching Anything

"Again I say unto you, that if two of you shall agree on earth as touching anything that they shall ask, it shall be done for them of my Father which is in heaven"
(Matthew 18:19)

Shortly after my father died, I moved from Oregon back to California to take care of my mother who was eighty-two and alone.

When I arrived back in California, one of the things I had to do to was sign up for a new health insurance company, as the one I had in Oregon did not provide good coverage in California. I chose a well-known HMO. They asked me if I would like to have a pre-coverage blood test as part of my physical. I asked them if it was required. They said no, but that it was a good idea. I opted for the blood test. Several weeks later I got a notice to come to the hospital.

I arrived, checked in, and was shown into a private waiting room. The doctor came in.

"Your blood test came back. You have Hepatitis C," he said.

I flashed back to Emilia in Oregon, and the letter she had got about her viral count. I was stunned; it had been thirty years since I had last shot drugs. I am sure I must have had a look of disbelief on my face.

"Didn't you know?" the doctor asked.

"No, I didn't. Is it curable?"

"We can cure it about 40 percent of the time at best," he said. "But the treatment has horrible side effects, and some people get suicidal from it."

I didn't know what to do.

"What would you do if it were you?" I asked him.

"I would take the treatment," he said.

After some reflection, I said, "All right then, let's do it."

On the drive home I was more than stunned. I had had blood tests several times over the last thirty years, but none of them had ever detected this. At home I got on the Internet and read everything I possibly could about Hepatitis C. I was completely ignorant. I learned it could be fatal, and that 7,500 people in the U.S. had died of it the year before. I looked into all the options: ozone therapy, herbal remedies, etc.

The hospital had also informed me that I was genotype one. It is supposed to be the hardest to treat. I learned online that it was a good idea to have a liver biopsy. I asked my HMO to do one, and they agreed. The results were less than encouraging. The biopsy determined that I had stage three liver disease. Stage four is the most advanced stage of liver disease. It is called cirrhosis. Once you get to stage four they say that your liver cannot recover, and I was almost there. The results caused the HMO to become more urgent in their request that I start treatment. They told me that if treatment didn't work they would put me on the liver transplant list. Suddenly, the possibility of death was looming over me.

A potential fatal disease was enough for me to seek some help; I contacted a church with a prayer ministry. I asked them to remember me in prayer. and agree with me in asking that I be healed. I also asked that my side effects from treatment be minimal. They agreed.

Treatment began and I waited for the horrendous side effects I had heard about to begin. Strangely, they didn't. I was spared the horrible rashes, anemia, and other side effects that cause some to abandon treatment.

People who receive treatment for Hep C are either responders or non-responders. Treatment is discontinued for those that don't respond at the twelve-week mark. I anxiously awaited the results of my twelve-week blood test. I called and was told that I was responding. I began to be hopeful.

Week after week, I reported to the nurse practitioner that I was not experiencing any side effects, and she was amazed. At some point I realized God had answered my prayer. I know, of course, that there will always be those who will attribute it only to medical science. But I know in my heart that God made it possible.

The year of treatment ended, and my blood tests were still normal. I went back for a one-year blood test, and the results were still normal. I was told that the liver can regenerate and that eventually my liver would go back to normal.

Chapter 14

Forgiveness

"If you forgive others for the wrongs they do to you, your Father in heaven will forgive you. But if you don't forgive others, your Father will not forgive your sins"
Matthew 6:14-5

Because of the hepatitis C treatment, I was not able to work for the first year I returned to California. I had applied for a reciprocal appraiser's license with the state of California. They required that I prove rehabilitation before they would issue it. While I was in southern Oregon, I had been approved to participate in a volunteer citizens' crime watch that patrolled the community to prevent crime. I was able to present letters of recommendation from people involved in the program as well as numerous letters from community members. I had been a real estate appraiser for twelve years in Oregon without a blemish on my record, not to mention the years I had been a licensed real estate agent in California. After a lengthy delay, the state of California decided I met the criteria of rehabilitation and issued a license.

I also decided to get a real estate salesperson's license again, as I had let my old one expire in 1993. I applied thinking it would be relatively easy. After all, I had held a salesperson's license previously, and also held valid Oregon and California real estate appraiser's licenses. The Department of Real Estate decided to do another investigation. It took the better part of a year. During that time I had people who wanted to give me their business, but I was unable to do it. It had been more than thirty years since my last criminal conviction, but I experienced difficulty getting licensed. Eventually, my salesperson's license was issued. After a year I applied to upgrade to a real estate broker based on my experience in real estate. After I passed the required exam, the state speedily issued a broker's license.

Outwardly, things were going fine, but inwardly I found I was still troubled. On occasion, I would become aware of subtle feelings of resentment lingering toward my mother. While I was at her home one day, her mere physical presence triggered subtle feelings of resentment in me. She was not doing anything. It was just unresolved anger from the long ago traumas of my past. As the years had passed, I had felt I was over it. In fact, I even told people that I was, and I believed it was so.

One day I went to a local barber shop for a haircut. A young man came into the barber shop with his young daughter as I sat in the chair. The daughter was about five years old. She just seemed so carefree and happy. I thought how I had once been just the same.

A few days later at church the subject of resentment came up. The minister asked me if I had given up resentment and anger. I think he suspected I hadn't. He did say I was getting better when I said I refused to put my mom in an old folk's home about six months earlier. I began to tell him about the barber shop incident and then yelled out, "How could someone do that to another person?" The anger surfaced. It was too obvious to deny.

At that point the minister said, "Ted, you haven't forgiven your mother." Then he said, "Your mom couldn't help what she did to you."

I said, "I realize that."

His reply was that I just knew it "intellectually" but didn't really know it. Then he said, "Ask God to show you that she couldn't help it. That is one prayer that God will answer and you will go free."

Even though it seemed strange (almost ridiculous) to ask God to show me that she couldn't help herself, I did just that. Alone in my room I knelt down, and asked God to show me that she couldn't help what she did to me. I asked in the name of Jesus Christ.

Several days later as I was driving, I began to remember an incident when I was about ten years old. I had been extremely cruel to another young boy. I don't want to go into the lurid details,but it was an extremely cruel thing to do and involved physical abuse. I could see at that time that something evil had taken me over and acted through me. In short, I had become just like the mother I hated when she beat me. I was beginning to see—not intellectually, but with deep understanding.

I talked with a staff member at the church about the meeting and what I had seen. When I described my being taken over by evil as a child, he said, "That's how it is with adults too." We also chatted about the compulsiveness of sin, and how many people think they choose to do evil. They see it as a sign of unwillingness to take responsibility for their actions to acknowledge their compulsiveness.

Through my own experience of being cruel and being taken over by a spirit of evil as a child, I slowly began to see that my mom was just as compulsive in her cruelty as I had been in mine. She couldn't help herself anymore than I could help myself. I don't know the details of her childhood, but she also was once an innocent child who had experienced her own traumas that made her a slave to sin. Somehow in seeing all this, I began to have compassion for my mom and let the resentment go. My prayer had been answered.

"And ye shall know the truth, and the truth shall set you free."
Jesus Christ, John 8:32

Chapter 15

BORN AGAIN

"Marvel not that I said unto thee, Ye must be born again."—John 3:7

For the next several years after God took away my resentment toward my mother life was better. But although the deep lifelong resentment was gone there was still more to unfold.

Sad to say, I fell to resentment. Really, the details are not too important. Basically, it involved a woman who wanted to be in charge, and control an event we were working on together. She took to telling lies to get her way. I resented her. And I found the resentment to have a devastating effect on me. Again, I turned to the staff member at the non-denominational church I had been attending. We spoke about it one day on the phone when I had called about another matter. The resentment was ongoing, and I just couldn't shake it.

"I thought I was beyond resenting someone like this," I said.

"Well, that's your new reality," he said.

"This resentment is really getting to me. I can't seem to shake it. I have resented my conscience before for showing me I was wrong to judge, but I'm not doing that now. I don't know what is wrong."

"You are resenting the resentment!" he said. "That's classic."

"What do I do about that?"

"Just realize it is all."

And I did.

Frankly, it was a little bit hard for me to understand, almost like someone shouting something to me from far away and I could only catch part of the words. But I sort of understood and pondered on it for a few hours. Amazingly enough, the realization worked its magic, and the next day the resentment with which I had been struggling was miraculously gone.

But there was a little more to realize—it happened a year or so later.

Again, it involved another minister at a different church from the one I usually attended. This particular minister does some radio counseling. I listened one day as he was talking to a woman who was calling him about guess what? a resentment.

"I am a born-again Christian for over fifteen years now, and I seem to have a problem and I want to be helped," the woman said. "I had a situation that went down really bad . . ."

The minister interrupted her. "Let me say this. If you think you're a born-again Christian, you don't need me. But if you have a problem, you're not a born-again Christian yet because a born-again Christian doesn't need any help from anyone. In other words, you have your Jesus. And if you have Him in you, there is nothing you can't solve. You were just about to say you had a problem with somebody."

"Yes."

"And then you got resentful toward them."

"Yes."

"But Jesus never got resentful toward people when they were sticking nails in Him and beating Him. Look how you can tolerate so little, such a slight, slight, how little you can tolerate. Where is your born-againness?"

"That's the thing . . . that's . . ."

"Let me show you. I think I can help your born-againness."

I was tracking with the conversation. I knew there were many people who thought they were born again but were not. But I was not prepared for what happened. The minister calmed the lady down, told her to close her eyes, and then told her she had to learn what forgiveness is. In that moment of prayer and stillness he said, "And in order to forgive, you have to have been forgiven and you have to know you have been forgiven. I have a message for you: God sent His only son and He said, 'If you believe that I am the one who has been sent, I only want you to know you have been forgiven.'"

Afterward, the lady said she opened her eyes and the room was brighter. She said she felt clean and her burdens were lifted.

The impact on me was profound.

I had been reading the Bible for more than thirty years. I knew there was something wrong, but I didn't quite know what it was. That weekend I told the minister at my church what I had witnessed (well, heard really). He said that was how the born-again experience was almost instantaneous. I told him I believed I was forgiven, but that I had doubts.

Several days later I asked God in prayer to be born again. To be honest, I had done it before, but apparently the timing was right this time. The next day I really began to believe that God had forgiven me for the terribly sinful life I had lived. Along with that came a tremendous sense of inner peace. It was no longer just intellectual. I really believed and knew God's love and compassion. The sins of the past no longer mattered. It was as if all my ugly sins had been written on a chalkboard and that the slate had now been wiped clean. I truly felt like I had a new life.

Now I know what it means to be born again.

• • • • • • • • • • • •

John 3:3

Jesus answered and said unto him, Verily, verily, I say unto you, Except a man be born again, he cannot see the kingdom of God.

Matthew 7:7

Ask, and it shall be given you; seek, and ye shall find; knock, and it shall be opened unto you.

APPENDICES

I

The late Dr. Malachi B. Martin was a Catholic exorcist and an advisor to three Popes. He sent me the following illuminating letter on February 20, 1997.

MALACHI B. MARTIN
116 EAST 63RD ST. #4B
NYC, NY 10021

February 20, 1997

Dear Ted,

Thank you for your most kind letter of December 24th. I'm glad you were able to listen to me on the Art Bell program. Please forgive my delay in replying. But since the publication of my novel, <u>Windswept House</u>, I have been kept busy with TV and radio shows. As a result, my volume of mail has considerably increased.

Yes, as I mentioned on Art Bell, possession can occur as a result of drug or alcohol addiction. It opens a doorway into the soul. The will becomes extremely weak due to its desire for a drink or drug. This weakness and compulsion for addictive chemicals allows evil spirits an avenue by which they may enter a person. This process may begin subtly, even gradually. As the disease of alcholism and addiction progresses, so too does the evil spirit strengthen its foothold in the unfortunate's soul. If you suspect your girlfriend is plagued by demonic forces, I always tell Catholics they must first contact the bishop of their diocese and thus have him investigate the case. Authority must at all times be followed. This is mandatory in cases of exorcism and I adhere to these principles myself. If you cannot find a bishop to cooperate then I suggest your girlfriend say the prayer of St. Michael the Archangel. It is a very powerful prayer. Also, have her invoke the most Precious Blood of Jesus Christ in times of trial and temptation. The Son of God died for her--he died for you and me--He will never fail her.

In the meantime, know that I shall keep the two of you in my Daily Masses and prayers. I ask that you pray for me as well as I once again take up the pen to continue work on my upcoming book. And please, be at peace. Our God is a merciful God of Love. He will look after you.

God Bless you always,

HMB Martin

Printed in the United States
By Bookmasters